90 Unfiltered Devotions for This Sometimes-Too-Serious Life

# GOODNESS GRACIOUS

HANNAH CREWS

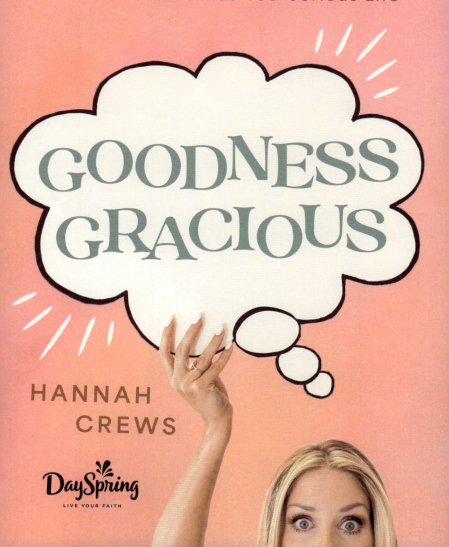

*Goodness Gracious: 90 Unfiltered Devotions for This Sometimes-Too-Serious Life*
Copyright © 2024 DaySpring. All rights reserved.
First Edition, February 2024

Published by:

21154 Highway 16 East
Siloam Springs, AR 72761
dayspring.com

All rights reserved. *Goodness Gracious: 90 Unfiltered Devotions for This Sometimes-Too-Serious Life* is under copyright protection. No part of this book may be used or reproduced in any manner whatsoever without written permission except in the case of brief quotations embodied in critical articles and reviews.

Unless otherwise noted, all Scripture quotations are taken from the Holy Bible, New International Version®, NIV®. Copyright © 1973, 1978, 1984, 2011 by Biblica, Inc.® Used by permission of Zondervan. All rights reserved worldwide. www.zondervan.com. The "NIV" and "New International Version" are trademarks registered in the United States Patent and Trademark Office by Biblica, Inc.®

Scripture quotations marked THE MESSAGE are taken from THE MESSAGE, copyright © 1993, 1994, 1995, 1996, 2000, 2001, 2002 by Eugene H. Peterson. Used by permission of NavPress. All rights reserved. Represented by Tyndale House Publishers, Inc.

Scripture quotations marked CEV are taken from the Contemporary English Version Copyright © 1991, 1992, 1995 by American Bible Society, Used by Permission.

Scripture quotations marked NASB1995 are taken from the New American Standard Bible®, Copyright © 1960, 1971, 1977, 1995 by The Lockman Foundation. Used by permission. All rights reserved. www.lockman.org.

Scripture quotations marked NLT are taken from the Holy Bible, New Living Translation, copyright © 1996, 2004, 2007 by Tyndale House Foundation. Used by permission of Tyndale House Publishers, Inc., Carol Stream, Illinois 60188. All rights reserved.

Scripture quotations marked GNT are taken from the Good News Translation in Today's English Version- Second Edition Copyright © 1992 by American Bible Society. Used by Permission.

Scripture quotations marked ESV are taken from the ESV Bible® (The Holy Bible, English Standard Version®) copyright ©2001 by Crossway Bibles, a publishing ministry of Good News Publishers. Used by permission. All rights reserved.

Scripture quotations marked CSB®, are taken from the Christian Standard Bible®, Copyright © 2017 by Holman Bible Publishers. Used by permission. Christian Standard Bible®, and CSB® are federally registered trademarks of Holman Bible Publishers.

Written by: Hannah Crews
Cover Design by: Greg Jackson

Printed in China
Prime: U1209
ISBN: 979-8-88602-392-3

# Contents

Foreword . . . . . . . . . . . . . . . . . . . . . . . . . . . . . 9
Introduction . . . . . . . . . . . . . . . . . . . . . . . . . . . 11
"Choose Joy?" Girl, Please . . . . . . . . . . . . . . . . . . . 12
Schmardashian Happiness or Jesus Joy? . . . . . . . . 14
Facebook Stalkers and Love Stories . . . . . . . . . . . 16
The Power of a Grateful Heart . . . . . . . . . . . . . . . 18
Not a Morning Person . . . . . . . . . . . . . . . . . . . . . 20
Praying for a Whale . . . . . . . . . . . . . . . . . . . . . . 22
A Spirit of Excellence . . . . . . . . . . . . . . . . . . . . . 24
Finding Favor . . . . . . . . . . . . . . . . . . . . . . . . . . 26
You Are an I.F.G. . . . . . . . . . . . . . . . . . . . . . . . . 28
They Were Cute, until They Opened Their Mouth . . . 30
Jenny Knows Best . . . . . . . . . . . . . . . . . . . . . . . 34
"Your Truth" Is Bologna . . . . . . . . . . . . . . . . . . . 36
On Time vs. Quality Time . . . . . . . . . . . . . . . . . . 38
Mirror, Mirror, on the Wall . . . . . . . . . . . . . . . . . . 40
Getting Rid of Stone Face . . . . . . . . . . . . . . . . . . 42
There's No Joy in Pain! Or Is There? . . . . . . . . . . . 44
Think Right, Talk Right, See Right . . . . . . . . . . . . 46
The Heart of an Energizer Bunny . . . . . . . . . . . . . 48
Go Big or Go Home . . . . . . . . . . . . . . . . . . . . . . 50
The Worst Day Ever . . . . . . . . . . . . . . . . . . . . . . 52
A Little Less Talk . . . . . . . . . . . . . . . . . . . . . . . . 56
Expectations, Schmexpectations . . . . . . . . . . . . . 58
Be a Barnabas . . . . . . . . . . . . . . . . . . . . . . . . . 60

| | |
|---|---|
| Vindication Is Inevitable | 62 |
| Comparison Is a Disqualifier | 64 |
| Yes, God Uses Imperfect People | 66 |
| Our Presence Affects the Present | 68 |
| Well, That Was Awkward | 70 |
| The Battle of the Overwhelm | 72 |
| The Most Important Devotion You'll Ever Read | 74 |
| You Do What We Doubt | 78 |
| No Shame in His Name | 80 |
| Never Early, Never Late | 82 |
| Silly Ol' Sheep | 84 |
| A Heavenly Mantle | 86 |
| Just One Praise Away | 88 |
| Absorbing the Word | 90 |
| There You Are | 92 |
| A "Word" for the Year | 94 |
| A Solution Seeker | 96 |
| Sticks and Stones | 100 |
| From Burnout to Balance | 102 |
| For Such a Time as This | 104 |
| Armor Up, Baby | 106 |
| P.U.S.H. | 108 |
| Please Like Me | 110 |
| Unlimited Creativity | 112 |
| Satan: The Ultimate Copycat | 114 |
| Good Fruit, Good Impact | 116 |
| Girl, Receive That Compliment! | 118 |

| | |
|---|---|
| Jesus Is My Homeboy | 122 |
| The Type of Comparison No One Talks About | 124 |
| Behind the Scenes | 126 |
| From In-Law to In-Love | 128 |
| "God, I Want Her Mermaid Fin." | 130 |
| Going Backward to Move Forward | 132 |
| Fear Is Not Yours to Carry | 134 |
| He Sees the Big Picture | 136 |
| You're Cordially Uninvited | 138 |
| The Most Important Devotion You'll Ever Read (Again) | 140 |
| Make Me a Vessel | 144 |
| Don't Compete, Complete!  | 146 |
| The Pursuit of Peace | 148 |
| A Way of Escape | 150 |
| A Well-Rounded Life | 152 |
| The Cycle Stops Here | 154 |
| The Seesaw and the Savior | 156 |
| "As for Me and My House," and Beyond | 158 |
| Worship Is Your Weapon | 160 |
| God, Where Are You? | 162 |
| An Orphaned Spirit | 166 |
| The Importance of Family | 168 |
| Why "Self-Love" Is Not the Answer | 170 |
| Spirit vs. Emotion | 172 |
| Social Media: Menace or Ministry? | 174 |
| The Three C's | 176 |

| | |
|---|---|
| Unclutter Your Heart | 178 |
| Boldness, Persecution, and X-rated Material | 180 |
| The Forgiveness Cure | 182 |
| When Nothing Is Going Right | 184 |
| Contentment: Our Gift to God | 188 |
| A Rich Spiritual Inheritance | 190 |
| As Good As It Gets | 192 |
| Things God Cannot Do | 194 |
| Gabbin' and Gossipin' | 196 |
| God, Why? | 198 |
| What Does 3-in-1 Even Mean? | 200 |
| Guarding the Gates | 202 |
| Charlie and the Smoky Hotel Room | 204 |
| A Life of Freedom | 206 |

# Foreword

"I got the joy, joy, joy, joy down in my heart! Where? Down in my heart! Where? Down in my heart!"

If you grew up as a church kid, I'm sure you sang right along to that tune. The innocence of childhood worship filled us with a profound sense of joy, seemingly bubbling up from the depths of our hearts. But as we've grown into adults, life's complexities sometimes make us question, "Where is it?" and we find ourselves still searching for this seemingly elusive joy. The same joy that once flowed so freely can feel like it's playing a never-ending game of hide-and-seek, rather than being a constant, steadfast companion.

So, what does walking in joy actually look like in our daily lives? Well, I believe it looks a lot like choosing to walk with Jesus each day. This choice isn't always straightforward; we may encounter resistance along the way. Yet, through every trial and triumph, it remains undeniably worth it! In Psalm 34, it tells us that when we turn to the Lord for help, we will shine with *radiant* joy! Friends, this is a promise! Now, it's time for us to learn how to truly walk in it. Can I get an amen?

*Goodness Gracious* is far more than just a cute devotional book designed to let you check off your "I spent time with Jesus today" box. It's a beautifully practical and hilarious tool that Hannah has crafted to help us draw near to Christ on the brightest of days, the darkest of nights, the mundane "meh" moments, and even the downright "bleh" days. Her writing has a remarkable way of making you feel seen and understood, all while gently challenging you to rise up. Trust me, my friends, you will laugh, cry, and grow through every single page. And by the end, you will be equipped to genuinely walk in the joy of the Lord, no matter what you might be walking through.

**Tori Masters**
Speaker, Podcaster, Content Creator
Connect with me on social media:
@torimasters
@talkswithtori
@morningswiththemasters

# Introduction

I have a confession to make:

I've never written a devotional before.

No, I'm not kidding. I'm just a goofy Texas girl who likes to watch *Seinfeld* reruns *and* only flosses if it's a dance move.

Wait, before you start digging for your return receipt, let me say this:

I know how you're feeling. The world today is over-the-top intense. The news is depressing, social media is soul-sucking, and godless filth is swirling around us like a flushing toilet bowl. Therefore, it's fair to say that "joy" is simply for naive absent-minded people who don't live in reality, right?! Goodness gracious.

Here is what I've learned. The most powerful thing we can do, especially in today's world, is to embrace the joy of the Lord. It's where our strength, endurance, and fortitude comes from. The presence of joy brings light, and where there is light, it is impossible for darkness to exist.

For the next ninety days, let's reclaim the joy of the Lord together. This journey will be unfiltered, lighthearted, and fun. In the process, I'd love to hang out with you on social media @hannahcrews.blog.

Ready? Let's do this, girlfriend!

*(You're cute when you smile, by the way.)*

*Hannah Crews*

# "Choose Joy?" Girl, Please.

*Rejoice always, pray continually, give thanks in all circumstances; for this is God's will for you in Christ Jesus.*
I THESSALONIANS 5:16-18

There was a point in time where the phrase "choose joy" was so gag-worthy to me. It felt overused, over-posted, so Christian girl cliché. "Choose joy? What, just pick it like a booger? Goodness gracious, stop it already."

But I had to sit back and reflect for a moment. Why was I triggered? Why doesn't the idea of choosing joy excite me and give me hope? I pinpointed two reasons: life was hard at the time, and I wasn't consistent in my personal relationship with Jesus. The problem wasn't the phrase, it was the turmoil going on inside of me.

I know "choosing joy" isn't that simple. It's not a light to switch from off to on. It's not the beginning of "Man! I Feel Like a Woman," where you instantaneously feel happier within the first three seconds. Oh, Shania. What a legend.

So, what's the secret? How can we choose joy in a way that actually works? Here are three keys to consider:

1) Choose Jesus. Choosing yourself, relationships, or temporary pleasures will always leave an empty hole.

True and unadulterated joy, in its purest form, is only found through Him.

2) Release offense, walk in forgiveness, and embrace surrender. When I shifted from a problem-focused to a solution-oriented attitude instead, it released so many emotional burdens. My heart became light, peaceful, and free.

3) Pray? Yes. Read your Bible? Double yes. Most Christians gloss over the number one key to experiencing supernatural joy, which is to open Scripture. Daily meditation on the living, breathing Word of God will not only increase joy, but it will also perform miracles by the renewing of your mind.

Once I started doing these things, everything changed. Soon enough, the "choose joy" phrase that was once so cringeworthy to me became noteworthy. I realized I must rejoice and pray even in the middle of my yuck circumstances, because that is His will for me. His actual will for my life is to "choose joy." And it is His will for yours too.

*Jesus, I thank You and praise You, even in the middle of my circumstances. I choose joy today. You died simply because You loved me, and that is enough for me to rejoice. Amen.*

# Schmardashian Happiness or Jesus Joy?

*If you serve Christ with this attitude [goodness, peace, joy], you will please God, and others will approve of you, too.*

ROMANS 14:18 NLT

I was watching a TV show that everyone's heard of, and I won't say it because it's slightly embarrassing, but it rhymes with "Schmardashians." Hey, stop giggling! Only God can judge me.

Anyway, in this particular episode, the phrase "I'm just trying to find my happiness" was repeated multiple times. We all know money can't buy happiness. But ain't it something how even people with billions of dollars can still experience unhappiness? I mean, goodness gracious, I would find it hard to feel unhappy while driving a Range Rover with a Barbie pink interior. But hey, that's just me. I've just never met a shade of pink I didn't like!

As I watched this episode, though, it made me think about the difference between happiness and joy.

Happiness is a feeling that wears off over time, but joy is a state of being one lives in. Happiness is an addicting yet fleeting euphoric high, but joy is a constant in one's character when they embody Christ's character. Happiness is based on what other people or material things can provide, but joy is something only God can provide.

This concept can be illustrated by two inflated balloons. One balloon is filled with air (happiness), and the other is filled with helium (joy). While the balloon of happiness appears to be full on the outside, the air it's filled with causes it to sink to the floor. The balloon of joy, however, not only appears full on the outside, but the helium of the Holy Spirit also causes it to stay afloat; and no matter how hard someone tries to bring it down, it will always rise back up.

God calls us to holiness, not happiness. With holiness comes obedience, with obedience comes faith, with faith comes hope, and with hope comes joy. Today, the Lord wants to shower you and your family (and even the Schmardashians) with a joy that can only come from Him.

*God, I recognize that the difference between experiencing happiness and joy is what I'm filled with. I want You to fill me up, Lord. I choose to delight in You today. Amen.*

# Facebook Stalkers and Love Stories

*Before I formed in the womb
I knew you.*
JEREMIAH 1:5

When I was nineteen, I got a weird Facebook friend request. This guy was a few years older than me, played the drums, and had a profile picture complete with spiky hair and skinny jeans. Not my type. He also had a prettier face than my girlfriends and I put together, which highly offended me. I decided that no matter what his intentions were, it was a big fat no from me.

Hold on, it gets weirder. Let's rewind about twenty-six years.

My mother had just given her life to Christ. One night at a revival service, she watched a woman go to the altar asking for prayers to conceive a child. The preacher prophesied over this woman and said, "You will have one boy and one girl." Six months later while grocery shopping, my mother saw that same woman across the aisle, glowing and pregnant. This miracle radically impacted my mother's life in a powerful way.

Fast forward again to the Facebook guy. I guess he got tired of me ignoring him, because he finally messaged and said, "Hey, I'm around a lot of chicks, but I'm really drawn to you. You need to call me." This dude was either hilarious or cocky, and curious me wanted to find out. So I called him. And goodness gracious, I liked him.

I told my mother about him, and of course we started stalking him on Facebook. While scrolling through his photos, we suddenly came across his family. The sound of my mother's gasp was quite dramatic and slightly excessive, but what she said next made me understand why. "Honey, that's the woman who prayed for God to give her children years ago, and the baby she was pregnant with at the grocery store was Blaine."

So yes, needless to say, I married Blaine. The Facebook guy.

God orchestrates great love stories. But more important than love with another person is your love relationship with Jesus. He is the Lover of your soul, pursuing you incessantly, and He will continue until you answer His call.

> Lord, I surrender my heart to You. I want to feel Your love like never before. Thank You for always pursuing me, even when I ran the opposite way. Draw me close today as I draw near to You. Amen.

# The Power of a Grateful Heart

*Let the peace of Christ rule in your hearts, since as members of one body you were called to peace. And be thankful.*

COLOSSIANS 3:15

For his sixth birthday, my son wanted a toy dinosaur. He had been talking about it for weeks, detailing the color, markings, and size as if he had an honorary master's degree in archaeology. Not to mention, the way he imitated the roar with such volume and aggression made me genuinely fear for his vocal cords.

Finally, the day came. He opened the gift, and his reaction freaked us out. With fists raised in the air, he yelled "yes!" multiple times and took laps around the house while screaming at the top of his lungs. The level of gratitude was both wild and hilarious.

Later that night, however, as I was putting him to sleep, he said "Mommy, that dinosaur wasn't the one I was talking about, but I love this one so much that I'm still happy." First of all, goodness gracious, I had no idea I still got it wrong. But even though it wasn't the dinosaur he had in mind, gratitude overflowed his heart so much that it didn't matter.

There is such power in a grateful heart. Believe it or not, a grateful heart results in inner peace with everything that goes on in our lives, both the good and the bad. How often do we forget to be grateful for our steady job, yet instead complain about not enough vacation time? How often do we forget to be grateful for our spouse, yet instead microscope every little thing they do wrong? How often do we forget to be grateful for good physical health, yet instead fixate on the superficial features we consider flaws?

Gratefulness allows us to focus on the gift rather than the grief. It is an eliminator of self-pity and a reducer of depression. It transforms us from being problem-focused to becoming faith-focused. When we practice gratefulness intentionally, even when we don't feel like it, it results in a deeper level of spiritual maturity. The simple fact that we have a Savior who *loved us enough to die* for us, gives us good reason to walk in gratitude forever.

> God, despite the hard things in life,
> I choose gratefulness. Always remind
> me of Your goodness so my heart
> can remain at peace. Amen.

# Not a Morning Person

*This is the day the L*ORD *has made.*
*We will rejoice and be glad in it.*
PSALM 118:24 NLT

When I first got married, my poor husband had no idea how much his new wife could sleep. And when I say sleep, I mean *sleep*. I could throw down about fifteen hours of uninterrupted triple z's with zero problem. It was impressive, I must admit. Borderline unhealthy but definitely impressive.

With that being said, I was never a morning person. If anyone tried to wake me up earlier than necessary, I'd emerge as an eye-booger monster with horrifying bed head and dragon-like halitosis. There was never anything attractive to me about rising before the sun; so when people talked about getting up early for quiet time with God, that was a hard no for me.

Obviously, life changes those cycles. Sleep schedules shift after having babies, rest patterns lessen with adulting responsibilities, and overly late nights became a thing of the past. The more I matured as a woman and the hungrier I became toward the things of God, I started to understand the value of being a morning person.

Three verses stand out to me the most:

Psalm 118:24. "This is the day the Lord has made. We will rejoice and be glad in it!" (NLT). This verse encourages me to look forward to mornings rather than dread them, because each day is a gift from God.

Lamentations 3:22-23. "The steadfast love of the Lord never ceases; his mercies never come to an end; they are new every morning; great is your faithfulness" (ESV). This verse gives me hope for a better day despite how bad the day was before.

Matthew 6:33. "Seek ye first the kingdom of God, and His righteousness; and all these things shall be added unto you" (KJV). This verse encourages me to reserve time with Him each day before anything else—before breakfast, work, or phone scrolling.

Rather than dreading mornings or having a constant case of "the Mondays," mornings have become a treasure. Now, my quiet time with Jesus is the most rejuvenating part of my day. No matter what your schedule looks like, carve out time for the One who loves you most!

*God, thank You for each day. My desire is to always set aside time for You. Amen.*

# Praying for a Whale

*In my distress I called to the LORD,
and He answered me.*
JONAH 2:2

We recently took a trip to Mexico. The locals told us it was whale season, and I really wanted that *Free Willy* moment. I wanted to see a whale do some sort of dramatic full-body leap complete with an upside-down belly flop landing. The likelihood was there, but the chances of catching a powerfully cinematic moment on camera was less likely.

The next day, while recovering from a stupid and very preventable sunburn, I decided to pray for it. I pulled out my phone and said, "Lord, let me see a whale. Let me see a humongous, massive whale just jump right in front of me. Let me see a big ol'…"

And then boom—it happened. The most beautiful whale shot up nose-first, did a half spin in the air, and landed with a grand slam splash finale. It was such a cool God-moment for me, but I also thought, "Goodness gracious, I can't imagine being stuck inside one of those like Jonah." Right then, the Holy Spirit reminded me that, actually, I have. Metaphorically speaking, of course.

Many times, in the midst of my own rebellion, God would allow desperate circumstances to swallow me whole in order to pull me toward obedience. He loved me enough to send whales (or trials) to draw me to my knees in humility. As painful as those lessons were, it was actually God's grace for me in action.

Maybe you're praying for a whale. Maybe you simply want to experience His majesty in a personal and intimate way. Or maybe you've been in a bad place and have found yourself in the depths of a dark and stinky situation. Either way, the wonderful thing about God is He knows exactly what kind of whale you need. Whether He sends a blessing or a lesson, God's intentions toward you are always good. He longs for you to seek Him, to keep a pure heart, and to live a life that is pleasing unto Him.

> God, send me a whale. Whatever You think I need, I trust You. Thank You for the blessings, and thank You for Your grace in the midst of the lessons. Amen.

# A Spirit of Excellence

*Whatever you do, work heartily,
as for the Lord, not for men.*
COLOSSIANS 3:23 ESV

Let's go back in time for a minute. The year is 1997, I'm in my second-grade classroom, and the teacher gave us a coloring assignment. More than anything, I wanted to be the first one to complete it. I scribbled as quickly as I could, ran to the table, and slammed the paper down as if I finished in first place on *The Amazing Race*. My classmates looked up, wide-eyed in awe. The rush of adrenaline was overwhelming. My ego skyrocketed. I proudly sat down with a cockeyed winner's grin. But little did I know, a humbling was about to come even faster than my pathetic scribble job.

Without missing a beat, the teacher walked to the back of the class, picked up my paper, and held it high up in the air. With an irritated snarl, she loudly announced, "Kids, this is what you're not to do. I will not tolerate sloppy work."

You could literally hear my pride deflating like a limp balloon. Tears streamed down my face. I dubbed her as my "least favorite teacher" for years. But goodness gracious, now that I'm an adult who understands the value of excellence, that lady was probably one of the best teachers I ever had.

When someone has a spirit of excellence, you can tell. It's evident in their appearance, in their home, in their workplace, and in their relationships. However, they not only show excellence with big things; they show it in little things. These people put shopping carts back, keep their grass mowed, pay bills on time, and exude responsibility in everything they do. In turn, they're often blessed. If you have ever looked at someone else's life and thought, "Wow, they're so lucky," the key might be simple—that person values excellence and properly stewards what they're given.

While excellence doesn't lead you to Christianity, embracing God's Word will lead you to a life of excellence. Seek Jesus; it will naturally set you apart, and it will make you want to do the next right thing.

*Lord, I want to live a life of excellence. Show me how to do that, in the big things and in the little things. Use me for Your glory in every area of my life. Amen.*

# Finding Favor

*Then Peter began to speak: "I now realize how true it is that God does now show favoritism but accepts from every nation the one who fears Him and does what is right."*

ACTS 10:34-35

Growing up, my mom prayed about everything. Even silly stuff! She'd pray for God to help find her car keys, she'd thank Him when they appeared, she'd pray for a close parking spot, and she'd thank Him when a front-row-Joe opened up. Sometimes I'd think, *Sheesh, Mom, just put your keys on the keyholder!* Or *Why don't you just show up earlier for a good parking spot?* However, I saw how those simple moments built my mom's faith. And, in turn, it greatly impacted mine too. The pattern here was simple: she prayed without ceasing, she kept her heart in a position that was pleasing to Him, and He'd show up for her—every single time.

Many try to capture favor through other people. It becomes a game of "who you know," networking with the "right people," or trying to force something to happen. However, when God's favor is involved, it always transcends any kind of favor man can provide. His favor doesn't depend on people, and His favor isn't forced; it's showered over those whose hearts are in right standing with Him.

Here are three keys to finding God's favor according to Scripture:

Fear God. This doesn't mean being scared or frightened, but rather having a strong desire to obey Him in all things. This kind of fear is healthy, pure, and pleasing in His sight.

Do what is right. Choosing to do the next right thing, in every situation, is paramount. And when your heart is in line with His, doing the right thing comes naturally.

Treat others well. Favor also follows those who treat others around them by the fruit of the Spirit. When you practice love, joy, peace, patience, kindness, goodness, faithfulness, gentleness, and self-control—yes, even with difficult Karens— God will always bless you in return. (Totally kidding if your name is Karen, by the way. I've got an Aunt Karen. She's nice.)

Chase the heart of Jesus. Because, goodness gracious, His favor is the sweetest.

> God, I want my heart to line up with Yours. Your favor is more valuable to me than man's. Help me as I strive to live in right standing with You. Amen.

# You Are an I.F.G.

*He said to them,
"Go into all the world
and preach the gospel to all creation."*

MARK 16:15

There's something about explaining my current job to people that has always made me feel a little wonkadoodle. There are so many mixed connotations to the word *influencer* that when someone new asks me what I do, I act like Homer Simpson who awkwardly glides backward into the bushes. I can never predict how people will respond—some are in awe of it, some make fun of it, some are interested in it, and some turn up their noses to it. I totally understand why too. The internet is weird.

But one Sunday at church, a visiting pastor said something that struck a chord with me. "No matter who you are," he said, "you need to be an I.F.G.—that's an influencer for God. Make Jesus famous everywhere you go." It was cute how he said "I.F.G." too, overly trying to sound hip and cool. Bless his heart.

Right at that moment, the most precious thing happened. I could physically feel my heart grow warm. It was like a blanket of peace covered me as the Lord whispered, "You are right where I want you to be. I have commanded my people to share the gospel in all corners of the world, and

I've given you a corner of the internet." At that moment, any wonky-feels I had toward my job completely vanished from my heart. Goodness gracious, Jesus is so sweet.

The main purpose of your life and mine, the double-triple-quadruple-infinity-plus-number-one-in-the-world purpose, is to proclaim the gospel and to love people. In order to do that, we have no choice but to accept the title of "influencers for God." Whether it's your kid's time-out corner, or a homeless street corner, or a corner of the internet, we have all been given a designated assignment to influence people for Jesus in some capacity. Wherever God is drawing you to, be obedient and embrace it unashamedly. Go to every corner He sends you, and make Jesus famous in the greatest way imaginable.

Do your thing, boo. You're an I.F.G.

> Jesus, I receive my designated assignment as an influencer for You. Draw me toward the corners in which You want to use me the most. I embrace wherever You call me, in the name of Jesus I pray. Amen.

# They Were Cute, until They Opened Their Mouth

*Charm is deceptive and beauty is fleeting, but a woman who fears the Lord will be praised.*

PROVERBS 31:30 CSB

Today's title either made you giggle, or it took you aback ever so slightly. I apologize; don't cancel me. I promise there is a point, and it points to Jesus; this is a devotional, after all!

For real though, hear me out. Have you ever known a person who was so attractive until you got to know them, and suddenly they went from super cute to yucky ducky? I went on a date with a guy like that once. Key word: ONCE. It's like I was looking at a handsome and fit Aladdin, but on the inside, he was just a greasy old Jafar.

I'm sure you've encountered someone like that. In this hurting and broken world, it's bound to happen. Who knows, maybe we've been "that person" in someone else's eyes before. But even in the ashes of our mistakes, God is famous for making all things new. Instead of putting a massive emphasis on outward beauty and physique, what if we allowed Jesus to prune our hearts in such a way that it caused us to become incredibly good-looking from the inside out?

While a body in motion stays in motion, the same goes with your spirit. Being fit spiritually involves daily time with God and is much more vital than being fit physically. Don't get me wrong, taking care of your temple is absolutely God's intention for you. However, the shape and composition of your body is the least interesting thing about you! You are known by your actions, and your heart is what you'll be remembered by. To make sure your spirit is the loveliest thing about you, do these things daily:

- Read Galatians 5:22-23. Find ways to embody these beautiful character traits throughout your day.
- Spend time in prayer. Ask God to sift through the depths of your heart and remove any ugliness that doesn't belong.
- Embrace forgiveness. Forgive others, forgive yourself. There is beauty in letting go.

And hey, you truly are stunning, my friend. The Jesus in you makes you that way!

> **Father, I want my heart to be the prettiest thing about me. Let it be more like Yours. Amen.**

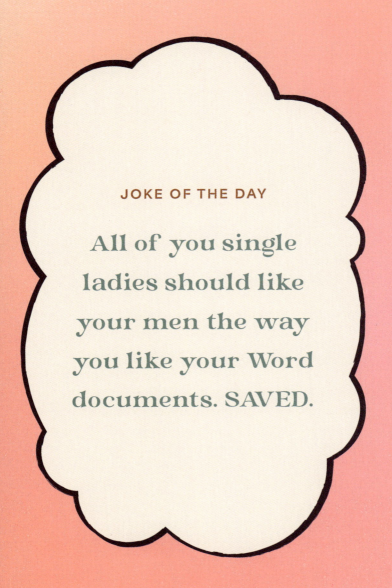

**JOKE OF THE DAY**

All of you single ladies should like your men the way you like your Word documents. SAVED.

# Jenny Knows Best

*"Yet not my will, but Yours be done."*
LUKE 22:42

There's always that one opinionated friend who has zero problem speaking her mind. For me, that's Jenny. She's embarrassingly honest, incredibly funny, and severely loyal; a combination that makes her charming enough to keep around. One day I was telling her about a new job I started, one completely different than anything I did before. After trying to convince her of my new "life purpose," she said this:

"I mean, it's just not what I envisioned you doing. But hey, I'm happy for you!"

Her response annoyed the fire out of me, and I just chocked it up as her being a little hater. However, after years of really high highs and really low lows with this particular job, I found myself burnt out, frustrated, and completely lost. It hit me—"Dadgummit, Jenny was right. I actually hate this. What in tarnation am I going to do now?" Once I surrendered my career path to the Lord and stopped trying to force a purpose that simply wasn't for me, everything changed.

If you've also found yourself in a season where you're floundering, lost, or feeling flat-out unfulfilled, implement these five things:

Read God's Word daily. When you understand who He says you are, it will bring you an overwhelming amount of clarity and confidence.

Ask God what His purpose is for your life. It truly is that simple. If you seek Him, you will find Him and in turn you'll find yourself again.

Remember, reevaluate, and refocus. Go back to your roots. Pinpoint your passions again. God didn't give you desires and dreams and gifts just for fun, He intended for you to live them out.

Talk to the Jennys in your life. Seek wisdom from those who know you and love you. If you're having a hard time identifying your gifts, ask them what they believe you're good at. Their answers might surprise you.

Operate in your giftings. Be obedient in this way. Realign your life with God's will rather than trying to force your own will upon God.

The Lord's plan for you is to be a vessel. Only you can do what He created you to do. Never underestimate that!

*God, I want to fulfill Your purpose for my life. Help me live that out today. Amen.*

# "Your Truth" Is Bologna

*"You will know the truth, and the truth will set you free."*

JOHN 8:32

It was one of those pretty quote graphics you see floating around on social media. "Just live your truth, boo," it said. The photo had dainty flowers, pretty colors, and minimalistic calligraphy lettering that could very well be your next inconspicuous tattoo. While the picture grabbed my attention, I strained to read it—and no, not because I have astigmatism. I was straining because, well, I just didn't get it. I gathered enough context to understand it probably meant to say stay "true to yourself" or "true to your convictions." But goodness gracious, when I spoke the phrase out loud, I felt like I had taken a bite of a six-day-old tuna sandwich. It just didn't settle well with me.

Years passed, and the phrase "live your truth" got more popular. However, if a person lives only by *their* truth, will it lead to them living within God's perfect will for their life? What does His Word say about this?

The Word of God is very clear when it describes what truth is. It says there is only one truth that sets us free, which is Jesus. It says Jesus is the Way, the Truth, the Life, and that no one can come to God except through Him (John 14:16).

It says that love doesn't rejoice in wrongdoing but rejoices in the truth (1 Corinthians 13:6).

So how do we share God's truth with those who are living their own truths? We do it with love. After all, isn't sharing about Jesus the most loving thing we can do for others? I think it would be just plain mean of us to deny the truth and allow others to believe that they are alone in this world and everything is on their shoulders. If we allow them to believe this lie, they will never get to experience Jesus, and they will never get to live God's best for them. After all, genuine fulfillment in life can only happen when we walk in perfect step with Jesus. We can never change the truth, but the truth can absolutely change us.

> God, I no longer want to live by my own rules or emotions or perspectives. If my truth isn't in line with Yours, I don't want it. May Your Truth set me free today, Jesus. Amen.

# On Time vs. Quality Time

*But seek first the kingdom of God and His righteousness, and all these things will be provided for you.*
MATTHEW 6:33 CSB

I don't enjoy being late to things. However, I also don't like to wake up early. When my daughter started ballet lessons, I set myself up for total failure by signing her up for the early-morning class. Goodness gracious, I should have known.

Sure enough, on ballet day one, I overslept. I jolted out of bed, started running to my daughter's bedroom, and almost tripped over my hideous oversized muumuu (What? It's comfortable sleepwear, okay?). I swung the door open so fast that it banged against her dresser, startling her out of a sound sleep. After fast-brushing her hair into a slicked bun, I threw her in the car like a basketball in a hoop and backed out of the driveway without looking. Of course, the city decided to do construction on our street that day, which resulted in my tires falling into a ginormous pothole. In total frustration, I did what any sane person would do: I punched the horn and held it down for a good three seconds.

Sinking back into my seat, I simmered down from the dramatics and started to examine myself. Tears began streaming down my cheeks, and I turned to embrace my little ballerina while praying for forgiveness. That moment taught me that being intentional with my time is much more important than compromising my character for the sake of being on time.

This reminded me of the story Mary and Martha, who were dear friends of Jesus. On the outside, Martha appeared productive, admirable, and servant-hearted. But on the inside, Martha was distracted, irritable, and anxious. She resented her sister Mary for not helping with chores and choosing to sit at Jesus's feet instead. However, Jesus was impressed by Mary's character the most. Mary didn't allow any outside circumstances to deter her from slowing down and focusing her undivided attention on the Savior of the world.

Let's be like Mary today. Let's not allow the busyness of life to come before spending intentional time with God. Take a deep breath in His presence, and give Him your undivided attention. Don't worry, the dishes can wait.

> God, I come before Your presence without distractions. Help my mind to be at ease as I seek You. Amen.

# Mirror, Mirror, on the Wall

*"For My thoughts are not your thoughts, neither are your ways My ways," declares the Lord.*

ISAIAH 55:8 ESV

Let's face it: mirrors are positively encouraging or blatantly horrifying. We can go from "goodness gracious, I look cute" in a dressing room, to thinking "never mind, I look like a potato" at home. A dimly lit mirror makes us believe our makeup is celebrity chic, but a brightly lit mirror can make us wonder if we actually belong in a carnival. I cannot tell you how many times I've freaked myself out in the morning, thinking a wigged-out lunatic must have broken into my house.

What we see shapes our perspective, or how we view things. However, because we are human, our perspective (unbeknownst to us) can be a deceiver. So often we see things in a way that is warped, distorted, or poorly illuminated due to our own shortcomings, hurts, and struggles. And if our perception toward something is even slightly skewed, it can lead us down a path of insecurity, judgmental thinking, and painful destruction. We must be careful with this. Focusing on a false reality long enough will eventually be seen as truth, and this will never produce God's best for us.

So how on earth do we get out of this carnival funhouse filled with wacky mirrors? How do we know if our perspective is right, or if it's totally and completely wonkadoodle?

Truth in our perspective is found by meditating on God's Word and spending quality time with Jesus. Doing this is like looking in a different kind of mirror: a magnifying mirror. It zooms into the depths of our hearts with honesty and conviction. It amplifies every micro-zit, mole hair, and skin flake on our character that simply doesn't belong. It reveals parts of our perceptions that might be true and other parts that are misconstrued. I don't know about you, but putting my pride aside long enough to look into a spiritual magnifying mirror isn't fun. But it helps me perceive myself, others, and life's situations in a way that lines up with Scripture.

God wants to beautify our hearts and clarify our points of view. The right perspective, in all areas of your life, will change everything.

> Lord, I ask that You adjust my mirrors. Help me see myself, others, and life's circumstances the way You do. Amen.

# Getting Rid of Stone Face

*Happy are those who hear*
*the joyful call to worship*
*for they will walk in the light*
*of your presence, Lord.*

PSALM 89:15 NLT

There is a term loosely used for people who have unintentionally "mean" facial expressions. But, since this is a nice Christian devotional, we're going to call it "stone face." Basically, people who suffer from "stone face" appear unfriendly and unapproachable when their face is innocently at rest. A friend of mine once said that when she saw me for the first time, she assumed I was a total snot simply because of my face. Of course, it took me aback, because I loved being her friend! However, when I reflect back on that time in my life, I was lacking joy severely. I was choosing to live beneath God's best for me, and it was showing in my countenance.

The more I read about the joy of the Lord, the more I learn about how physically transformative it is. And when I encounter people now, it's easy to discern who embodies joy simply by the way they carry themselves. A joyful spirit is in direct proportion to what's going on behind the scenes. Oftentimes, people who exude joy are faithfully intimate with God, and it's written all over their faces. These people rejoice always, even amid suffering, and they live as victors rather than victims. No matter what is going on in their lives, their obedience and hunger for God bring them joy that transcends even the deepest of pains.

Joy is more than a smile. It's an internal belief that God is your Shelter, Rock, Foundation, Comforter, and Savior. Joy is also magnetic; people will be drawn to you, which gives you an opportunity to be a witness for Christ.

While it's easy to blame difficult people or difficult circumstances for our lack of joy, the issue usually lies within ourselves. Allowing offense, pride, envy, worry, or bitterness to rule our mind and emotions will prevent Jesus from shining through. Be honest today; identify the joy-blockers within your own heart. Embrace forgiveness, gratefulness, and peace. Live in such a way that others can't help but wonder what you have!

> God, I want to embody joy. When others see me, let them see You. I desire to be a magnet for Your kingdom today. Amen.

# There's No Joy in Pain! Or Is There?

*Rejoice in the Lord always.*
*I will say it again: Rejoice!*
PHILIPPIANS 4:4 CSB

I recently picked up pickleball. If you've never played it, it's super fun. Once I finally got the hang of it, I joined a weekly women's league. However, I must have been doing something weird every time I played, because I started feeling discomfort in my lower back. One day, while taking care of my 97-year-old bedridden aunt with Alzheimer's, I bent down to pick up something off the floor, and when I stood up, my back gave out. It was excruciating. I screamed and collapsed, barely breathing. After about twenty seconds of me being all drama-sauce and making a bunch of "oo-oo-aa-aa" monkey sounds, I heard an elderly voice from the back bedroom. With a darling and shaky southern accent, my aunt yelled, "Hello? Who goes there?"

I lost it. The way she said "Who goes there?" was so old-fashioned and cute and innocent that it made me laugh uncontrollably. Mind you, I was unable to move, yet I was cackling as if I hadn't just slipped a disc. I thought to myself, "Are you crazy, Hannah? Why are you finding this scenario so funny in such a painful moment as this?" But the answer was simple: the joy of the Lord was sustaining me!

In life, we will feel both physical and emotional pain. It's inevitable; things happen that we don't ask for. And even though joy doesn't eliminate our pain, it will give us the endurance to go through it with grace. God doesn't want us to set up camp and sulk in the valley, He wants us to pass through it without fear. When we stop wearing our condition as an identity and start embracing God's identity amid our condition, we will walk in victory and become a beacon of hope and joy to everyone around us.

You are only as strong as your level of joy, because the joy of the Lord is your strength. When your joy in Jesus increases, your strength through pain increases. No matter what you're going through, choose joy in Jesus today. It is the key that will sustain you.

> God, in the middle of my pain, I want Your joy to strengthen me. I desire to be a living testimony of Your goodness in all circumstances. Amen.

# Think Right, Talk Right, See Right

*Be careful how you think; your life is shaped by your thoughts.*
PROVERBS 4:23 GNT

Have you ever assumed something and eventually realized you were way off? Yup, same here. I'll always regret the time when I made fun of my friends for loving boba tea. To me, without ever trying it, I knew it was disgusting. "Have fun drinking your boobie tea," I'd tell them. "Goodness gracious, those little balls on the bottom look like mini rabbit turds," I joked. That is, until one brave day, I decided to try it—and oh my heavens, my life changed. After tasting its smoothie goodness with a side of tapioca fun-ness, I realized that my assumptions about boba tea were completely wrong. If I could apologize to a drink, I absolutely would. But I couldn't, so I just apologized to my friends.

Because my thought process was off, it led to my words being off, which led to the way I perceived things to be off. Come to think of it, this happens to us quite a bit in life. When we think wrongly about something, we will speak wrongly about it, and the way we see it becomes very misaligned. This goes for our interactions with people, our circumstances, and even our relationship with God. Let's break it down:

Think Right: We must guard our hearts, first, by thinking right. When our minds are renewed, we think more like Jesus, which prevents us from believing lies. Our character is, mainly, defined by our thoughts.

Talk Right: The things we speak are direct correlations to what is going on in our hearts. Whatever our hearts are dwelling on will eventually become vocalized. Because the human mind is fickle, it is a dangerous thing to mistake "speaking without thought" for "speaking the truth." Therefore, examine your thoughts and your heart above all else before using your words in any situation.

See Right: When we think the way Jesus thinks and talk the way Jesus talks, we will see things the way Jesus sees. This causes healing instead of division and peace instead of turmoil. If your thoughts, words, and perceptions are steadfast, God will keep your life in perfect peace.

*God, renew my mind, my words, and my perceptions today. I want my character to be aligned with Yours. Amen*

# The Heart of an Energizer Bunny

*But we rejoice in our sufferings, knowing that suffering produces endurance, and endurance produces character, and character produces hope.*

**ROMANS 5:3-4 ESV**

One of my favorite comedic movies of all time is *Pitch Perfect*. There's one part where Fat Amy tells her friends, "Oh no, I don't do cardio." The way she says it is so funny, so definitive, and so stinking relatable. I get it; because every time I do cardio, it's dreadful. I can't breathe, sweat beads up in the most ungodly of places, and I want to quit halfway through every single time. However, after recovery, I feel like the Energizer Bunny. I can think clearer, I have more endurance, and my mood is boosted for the remainder of the day.

In the Bible, the woman with the issue of blood experienced something dreadful of her own. However, hers wasn't a thirty-minute cardio blast; it was twelve years of a hopeless condition with no end in sight. But, this chick never gave up. She endured, believed, and fought her way through the crowd just to grab a touch of Jesus's garment. Because of her faith, and because of her Energizer Bunny heart, she was healed.

I don't know what kind of trial you're walking through right now, but I do know you have the endurance for it. God has put His eternal battery within you. The same power that keeps the world spinning and the same power that raised Jesus from the grave is the same power that lives within you. Your heart and your spirit, despite every emotional hardship, will never quit on you. You were designed to persevere, to be healed in the process, and to be a mighty force for the kingdom of God.

Let this knowledge rearrange your thoughts and attitudes about your current circumstances. Let it bring you a peace you never thought possible. Refuse to be provoked when things get hard; be still, allow every negative emotion to pass without consuming you. With this type of surrender and self-control, you will gracefully conquer any tragedy, rejection, irritation, strife, or pain that comes your way. With faith, your heart will not only endure, but it will also be healed.

> Jesus, today, I'm touching the hem of Your garment. I have faith that You will help me endure everything in my life. Amen.

# Go Big or Go Home

*If you then, though you are evil, know how to give good gifts to your children, how much more will your Father in heaven give the Holy Spirit to those who ask Him!*

LUKE 11:13

After years of living in tiny apartments, Blaine and I were ready for a single-family home. Our poor neighbors were probably itching for us to leave too. Paper-thin walls sure make it hard to sleep when there's a newborn baby next door screaming bloody murder every hour of the night. I'm shocked the cops were never called.

After looking around, we found a house. It was beautiful, functional, perfect for our growing family; and goodness gracious, this momma wanted it, *bad*. However, someone beat us to the punch, and we were second in line. *Womp, womp, womp.*

The scenario seemed bleak, but we started praying *big*. We prayed that God would grant the desire of our hearts. We prayed that He would somehow, someway, draw the landlord's eyes toward our application. Sure enough, one week later, we got the call: our prayers were answered, the owner denied the first application and chose us. I literally jumped and squealed and danced like Elvis in celebration.

We were in awe of how God granted us favor despite such unfavorable circumstances!

Sometimes it's hard to believe that God truly listens to the things we ask for, *but He does*! He wants to show up in ways that are beyond our wildest dreams. He wants to prove that He can do exceedingly and abundantly above anything we could ask or think.

In fact, did you know that praying limited prayers is an insult to our Almighty God? Refusing to ask Him for big things is basically saying, "I don't believe You can do that, therefore I won't even ask." Bologna snot! He is more than able, and it tickles Him pink to hear us ask for the most gigantic, humongous, colossal requests.

No, God is not a genie. But He is a loving Father who desires to bless His children. Asking God for the miraculous puts our faith on display; therefore, be unafraid to go *big* when you pray!

> God, I pray for the miraculous today.
> And if it is Your will, then guide
> me on what to do next. Amen.

# The Worst Day Ever

*This is the day the Lord has made;*
*let's rejoice and be glad in it.*
PSALM 118:24 CSB

This is just the worst day ever!" my 6-year-old son wailed. We had just pulled into the parking lot of our local pizza arcade, only to discover it was closed due to construction. His dreams were shattered. This meant he couldn't play rigged games with a greasy marinara sauce smile in a germy room that smells like dirty socks. So, yes, naturally for him, this was the worst day ever.

Fast forward to a different day. "I can't. I just can't with today," I said in frustration. It was one of those days where nothing went right. I woke up with a massive zit on my chin, got in a stupid argument with my husband over if humans can use dog shampoo, and found a massive hole in the crotch of my leggings (*after* my Pilates class was already over). So, yes, naturally for me, it felt like the worst day ever.

Is it ever *really* "the worst day ever" though? Goodness gracious, of course not! Negative emotions and flawed perspectives can overexaggerate the way we feel about many things. However, each day is a masterpiece created by God specifically for us. The day isn't what is bad; rather, our imperfect responses can cause things to feel worse than it actually is. When we release control to God on days like this instead of allowing our flawed feelings to dictate our reactions, He reveals His goodness in the middle of the mess.

When you start to feel exasperated, disappointed, or crushed during a given day, do these things:

- Open up God's Word. The living, breathing Word of God renews the mind in a powerful way. It will loosen the grip we have on our flawed perspectives and shift our focus toward things that are good and true.
- Examine your own heart. Let go of self-centeredness, offense, and anger. Embracing humility and forgiveness brings overwhelming joy!
- Find a way to serve others without expecting anything in return. Choosing to be a blessing allows God to move freely in your life and in the lives of others.

His plans for you, today and forever, are always good!

> Lord, I choose to rejoice in this day You created. No matter what has happened, I lift my hands in gratefulness and total surrender. Keep refining me. Amen.

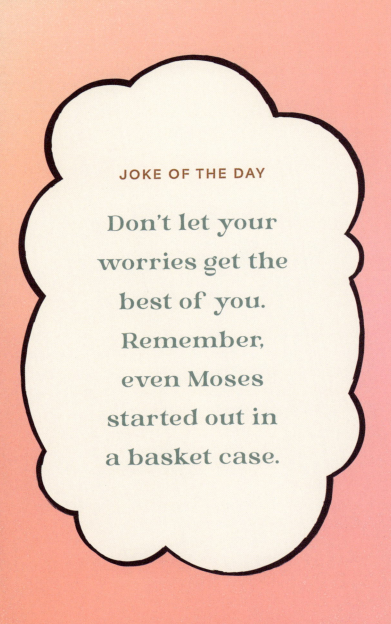

**JOKE OF THE DAY**

Don't let your worries get the best of you. Remember, even Moses started out in a basket case.

# A Little Less Talk

*Be still, and know that I am God.*
PSALM 46:10

Recently, I went shopping and ran into someone I had met before (multiple times, apparently). She was so sweet, so kind, and clearly had a great memory. I, on the other hand, was experiencing the biggest brain fart of my life. With a forced smile and a clinical case of airheadedness, I did what any ditzy chick would do: only talked about myself. It was safer this way, foolproof, a way to cope with my own embarrassment. My internal dialogue was brutal: *Dude, go take some fish oil or something, because your memory is like Dory's from* Finding Nemo *right now.* Of course, I remembered exactly who she was as I walked to my car. *See? If you had only shut up for two seconds and let her talk, you would have remembered her,* I told myself. Goodness gracious, how mortifying.

This encounter made me realize something. How often is it, when we pray, we're so busy talking about our own lives and our own problems, that we fail to remember who we're talking to? Instead of getting to know the God of the universe and allowing Him to speak, we monopolize the conversation as if the universe revolves around us.

The best way to get to know our precious heavenly Father is in the stillness. Sitting with Him in silence gives Him the opportunity to speak. When we release control in our prayer life, He reveals Himself mightily and steers us in the right direction. Practicing silence in prayer helps us to "practice the pause" in other areas of life—we will start to pause before assuming, pause before responding, pause before acting. Just like exercise strengthens our physical muscles and allows our body to operate at its best, silence before God strengthens our spiritual muscles and allows His character to shine through us.

Find a place of serenity and solitude in your home. Remove all distractions, take deep breaths, and fix your eyes on Jesus. Ask Him to speak to you. Imagine His arms wrapped around you. Focus on His mercy, glory, grace, and majesty. Oh, what a good friend we have in Jesus!

> God, I'm here. Meet me in the stillness, speak to me in the silence. I am giving You full control, and I want more of You in this moment. Amen.

# Expectations, Schmexpectations

*Now to Him who is able to do immeasurably more than all we ask or imagine, according to His power that is at work within us.*

EPHESIANS 3:20

"Expect the worst, but hope for the best," they say. Most times, I do. However, on this particular day, it was a dumpster fire.

The excitement surged through my veins as they clipped the microphone on my white jumpsuit. The lights were bright, the teleprompter was cued up, and the cameramen were counting down. It was my first time being a special guest on a comedy show, and it truly felt like a dream come true. However, as the show progressed, it took an unexpected turn. The host's jokes got raunchy, my laughs morphed into mortified chuckles, and the cameras zoomed in on my wide-eyed reactions. Needless to say, I should've done more homework on what to expect before showing up.

Expectations are a great thing for accountability in relationships. However, unmet expectations can lead to offense and division, which is not God's best for any of us. I came across an excellent video done by Jason Laird, founder and CEO of Sidecar Leader, that put things into perspective. Expectations can become unhealthy due to these four reasons:

- **Unconscious expectations.** When you're unaware you have this expectation of someone to begin with.
- **Unspoken expectations.** When you're aware of your expectations, but you haven't communicated this with the other person.
- **Unrealistic expectations.** When the expectation you have for someone is beyond their capability to meet or perform in the first place.
- **Unagreed-upon expectations.** When you're aware of your expectation, it's realistic, you've verbalized it, but that person hasn't agreed to fulfill it.

I know many times in my life, I've been guilty of at least one of the above, if not all. It's so important for us to be conscious of our expectations, verbalize them out loud, evaluate if they're realistic or not, and make sure they are agreed upon. One thing is for certain, though: our God will always exceed our expectations far more than we could ever ask or imagine. Therefore, He will always pull through for us, no matter what.

> God, help me have healthy expectations of others. Even if things don't go the way I anticipate, I know I can always expect wonderful things from You. Amen.

# Be a Barnabas

*Each of us should please
our neighbors for their
good, to build them up.*

ROMANS 15:2

I have these recurring nightmares that are actually quite hilarious. In these dreams, I find myself on stage at a dance recital. However, I'm also completely butt-naked, lady bits flailing in the wind, and have no idea what the dance is.

I believe this stems from a real-life circumstance that happened when I was younger. Not only did I have the hardest time remembering each eight-count during my dance recital, apparently my underwear was peek-a-booing through my costume the entire time. Goodness gracious, so mortifying.

After the show, one of the dance instructors, Martha, walked up to me and did something completely unexpected. She said, "Hannah, I just have to tell you, I'm really impressed with the technique you used during that performance! Great job, honey!" In an instant, every ounce of embarrassment inside of me completely vanished, and peace flooded over me in a way I will never forget. Martha's words allowed me to experience the power of what a simple act of encouragement can do for a lowly heart.

In the Word of God, Barnabas was just like Martha. He

was a known encourager. He celebrated successes with others, he was constantly pointing out the good, and he encouraged them to remain true to Jesus. While most people want to be center stage and on the receiving end of accolades and praise, our job is to be just like Barnabas—a ceaseless encourager. We are called to lift people out of dungeons of despair, pull them out of self-made pits, and inspire them to pursue the next right thing.

If we are constantly fishing for compliments, we will always be left with the need for more. However, when we allow our source of encouragement to come from Christ, it overflows our cup and allows us to be a Barnabas for others. Martha's words allowed me to experience the power of what a simple act of verbal encouragment can do for a lowly heart.

> God, I want to be a Barnabas today.
> Give me an opportunity to see something
> good in someone and to verbalize it
> with courage and kindness. Amen.

# Vindication Is Inevitable

*Be still before the Lord and wait patiently for Him; do not fret when people succeed in their ways, when they carry out their wicked schemes.*

PSALM 37:7

It always hurts when you're lied about, misunderstood, or the topic of untrue gossip—doesn't it? I remember times in high school when the experiences of "mean girls" were so intense, they would make me want to vomit (preferably in their hair, but I refrained). At that age, all you want is to be loved and accepted by your peers; and when the opposite occurs, the desire to explain or avenge yourself burns inside of you. You feel angry, devastated, and a deep longing all in one. Thoughts of "I just want them to like me," "That's not what happened," or "How can I convince them of the truth?" are all-consuming.

One thing I've learned is this: if my heart was wrong or if my actions were out of line, God always brought me back to my knees in repentance. However, if my heart was pure and my actions lined up with truth, no matter what others said about me, I was able to keep moving forward. Not to mention, I cannot count how many times, even years later, the "mean girls" would reach out to apologize and request forgiveness for any lies or torment that transpired during years of immaturity.

The Lord is a pro at examining every heart with a fine-toothed comb—yours, mine, and theirs. He sees truth with a perfect perception. No matter the time frame, the result remains the same: God always brings the truth to light.

It's so important for us to examine our own hearts, motives, and intentions during painful experiences with other people.

Friend, Jesus will make every wrong, right. He'll correct you when necessary, and He'll correct others when needed. Rest and be at peace. He's got it under control!

> God, I know that You are in full control of every painful situation. No matter what, keep my heart in line with Yours. Amen.

# Comparison Is a Disqualifier

*"Indeed, the hairs of your head are all counted. Do not be afraid; you are worth more than many sparrows."*

LUKE 12:7 CSB

I ran track in high school, mainly competing in relays and sprints. I'd go to my mark, get set, and blast off with force when the gun went off. But this one particular race, I started to feel this stupid ugly monster slowly creep up on me. *No, silly, I'm not referring to the runner next to me as a stupid ugly monster. That would be rude.* I'm referring to the voice of comparison that tried to break my spirit as I was falling behind. *You suck, Hannah. Loser with a capital L. Ew, why are you still running?* Now that was rude.

I wish I could share a happy ending and tell you that I rose above it and won the race after all. Nope, negative. Comparison ate me alive. My coach knew it too, because when I crossed the finish line, her stern glare spoke volumes and scared the living daylights out of me.

Track coaches are infamous for saying, "Never look over your shoulder." Looking to the person to your left or right slows you down, discourages, frightens, and even can cause stumbling and injury. Furthermore, if you step into someone else's lane, you will be disqualified completely.

For coaches, one thing matters most: a runner who works hard and keeps their eye on the finish line.

In life, you're running in your own lane. However, competing and comparing yourself to others beside you is the opposite of what God intended. He crafted you and gifted you and anointed you for a lane no one else can occupy. Why disqualify yourself by shifting your eyes toward someone else's race, or by trying to step into their lane?

Today, look up in the stands. You have a heavenly Coach who made you uniquely and magnificently, as well as an entire cheering section of family and friends who love you and are in constant awe of what God is doing through you. But if you have been guilty of comparison, take heart. The loudest cheers are always for the runner who stumbled, fell, bled, and fought to cross the finish line. Keep your eyes on Jesus despite the wounds. Your testimony of victory will result in the entire stadium erupting in praise.

*Father, deliver me from comparison. May it no longer steal my joy. Thank You for making me, me. Amen.*

# Yes, God Uses Imperfect People

*Therefore, there is now no condemnation for those who are in Christ Jesus.*

ROMANS 8:1

Ever feel so guilty about something that it suffocates you? Goodness gracious, how I can relate, my friend. Thoughts of "Why did you do that, ya nincompoop?" fill the heart and mind. You wish it was just a bad dream, where you can wake up with relief knowing it wasn't real.

There was a period in my life where I was so broken, I didn't feel worthy enough to worship God. I felt like He could no longer use a shameful mess like me. I told myself that a girl with my kind of baggage isn't worthy of being used by the Lord. Even though my repentance was sincere, I still saw myself as damaged goods.

But God. But the cross, where He bore it all!

Jesus doesn't require us to be faultless or pain-free in order to step into His presence. In fact, there is nothing we can ever do to make Him love us more, and there is nothing we've ever done that will make Him love us less. It is in His presence where we can expect forgiveness, express sorrow, and experience a completely transformed life.

The Bible is full of men and women who have made mistakes. However, despite it all, God used them anyway.

Here are just a few examples:

Abraham lied.

Peter denied Jesus.

Noah got drunk.

Jonah ran from God.

Jacob was a cheat.

Elijah was suicidal.

Job went bankrupt.

Miriam was a gossip.

Gideon was insecure.

Sarah was impatient.

Jeremiah was depressed.

Thomas doubted Jesus.

Moses was a murderer.

David committed adultery.

Paul slaughtered Christians.

Martha was a worrier.

The Samaritan woman was divorced.

Rahab was a prostitute.

If God can use them, why can't He use you? He loves you, even when you feel nothing but shame. He is still pursuing you, even in moments where hiding feels safer than being seen. We don't worship Him because we are good; we worship Him because He is good! Whatever heaviness you have been carrying, today is the day the shame game ends.

*Jesus, thank You for the cross, where You bore my shame. Heal my wounds, forgive my past. Today, I receive newness in You. Amen.*

# Our Presence Affects the Present

*Know this, my beloved brothers:
let every person be quick to hear,
slow to speak, slow to anger.*
JAMES 1:19 ESV

Confession time: my husband and I enjoy pizza arcade nights with the fam (don't laugh). Seriously though, it's fun to watch our kids have a blast, and the childhood nostalgia makes it a joyful experience. One day (since I'm clearly a mature adult), I hopped on a Jurassic Park game and started shooting some virtual velociraptors. Suddenly, a loud, curly-headed kid ran up to my vibrating chair and grabbed the toy gun from my hand. "I want to play! It's my turn!" the little guy said. His dad quickly pulled him away, but about ten seconds later, the same thing happened. "It's MINE! Get UP!" the kid aggressively shouted. He was zeroed in, focused, and wanted to play that dinosaur game, like *now*. At first, I started feeling angry. *Listen, bro, can I just be a kid for like three minutes?* I thought. But thankfully, grace swelled in my heart; since I'm a parent myself, I knew the frustration that father was feeling. Goodness gracious, raising kids can be hard!

How often, though, do we forget how our presence affects those around us? We get so wrapped up in our own circumstances that we forget how we share space with others. When we're loud in places where silence is appropriate, it affects those around us. When we're foolishly arguing in the comments section on social media, it affects those who read from afar. When we rudely express displeasure about our meal at a restaurant, it affects those sitting beside us.

In order to be a good example as believers, we must be aware of the position of our hearts. When we think before we speak, listen before we respond, and practice self-control in every circumstance, peace thrives within us and those around us. Of course, there is no better example of this than Jesus. His presence always left people feeling better than they did before. Thankfully, our heavenly Father loves us so much that there's grace when we mess up. Use today as an opportunity for your presence to bring life to those around you!

> God, I want to be a walking example of joy and peace. Help me to be conscious of everything I say and do. Amen.

# Well, That Was Awkward

*Now the word of the L*ORD *came to Jonah the son of Amittai, saying, "Arise, go to Nineveh, that great city, and call out against it, for their evil has come up before me." But Jonah rose to flee to Tarshish from the presence of the L*ORD*. He went down to Joppa and found a ship going to Tarshish.*

JONAH 1:1-3 ESV

I can only imagine how awkward it was for Jonah in the Bible. God told him to preach in the gospel in the pagan city of Ninevah, but instead, freaked-out Jonah cowardly boarded a ship going in the opposite direction. This led to a massive sea storm, which resulted in him being tossed off the boat, which led to him being swallowed by a whale. After spending three helplessly awkward days in a smelly belly, the whale vomited him out. Covered in fish slime and overwhelmed by embarassment, Jonah finally agreed to obey God and travel to Nineveh. Goodness gracious, how awkward is that!

Let's be real, though. Life can be awkward! We must face things we'd rather not, experience feelings we'd rather bury, have conversations we'd rather ignore. Suppressing it seems easy, but it will also suppress any growth God is trying to do in our hearts and lives.

I can only imagine how awkward Jonah must have felt that day. Being swallowed alive is quite the wakeup call, don't you think? Goodness gracious, try explaining that story to your family and friends!

Of course, I'm giving a lighthearted interpretation of it. I'm sure it was an excruciating experience. Obedience to God, no matter how awkward or challenging it is, always results in blessing. If you've been avoiding something that God has called you to do, take courage and act in faith. The uncomfortableness is temporary, but His promises are forever!

> God, may Your will be done in my life. No matter how weird or awkward I think it may be, I desire to obey You and grow personally, relationally, and spiritually. Amen.

# The Battle of the Overwhelm

*God is our refuge and strength,
an ever-present help in trouble.*

PSALM 46:1

In the process of writing this devotional, I ignorantly agreed to sign my kids up for like forty-two different extracurriculars. Unbeknownst to me, this was to become the most time-consuming season of my life. The closer the book deadline approached, the more intensely my attention was pulled in other areas—household chores, projects for work, providing emotional support for others, raising kids joyfully, shaving my legs, showering, being a hottie for the hubby, you know. All things that require intentional time and lots of energy.

I began to beat myself up: "How arrogant of you to think you can write a whole *book*, plus try to be everything for everyone at the same time. There's no way you can do all of this." While sitting in the parking lot of Michael's after racking up a $100 tab for my daughter's school project (one of those that just ends up in the trash anyway), I hit a breaking point. I closed my eyes and yelled, "God, I need *help*!" Being the gracious, patient, and compassionate sweetheart He is, Jesus whispered exactly what I needed to hear:

"Don't worry, daughter. I will rescue you."

Air returned to my suffocated lungs, and peace poured over me like a soothing balm. Goodness gracious, He is so wonderful.

You might be reading this today in the middle of your own overwhelming battle. It may be a heartbreak, a health crisis, a demanding schedule, marital problems, parenting struggles, or even a critical inner voice. Whatever it is, these things are for sure:

Our God is a *time restorer*.

Our God is a *strength provider*.

Our God is a *situation fixer*.

Our God is a *rescuer*.

Just when we think we can't handle it anymore, our vulnerable surrender allows Him to step in at just the right moment.

Open up to your Savior today. Vocalize everything that is stressing you. He desires nothing more than to minister to you; let His supernatural peace whisper over every overwhelming aspect of your life.

> God, rescue me in the midst of my overwhelm. Remind me continually that I can do all things through Christ who gives me strength. There is nothing too big for You, and because You love me, I know everything is going to be okay. Amen.

# The Most Important Devotion You'll Ever Read

*If you openly declare that Jesus is Lord and believe in your heart that God raised Him from the dead, you will be saved.*

ROMANS 10:9 NLT

Goodness gracious! You've been reading this devotional for an entire month (or maybe you've read at your own speed, or maybe you just opened the book to this page)! Whatever the case, thanks for being here with me today. You're a doll.

My prayer is that God continues to show you how real He is and how much He loves you. In fact, He loves you so much He sent His only Son to pay the price for you. Everything you've ever done, every flaw and fault and failure, Jesus bore it on the cross. He did it because it was the only way for all of us to experience eternity with Him, if we choose to.

God's Word says if you confess with your mouth that Jesus is Lord and believe in your heart that God raised Him from the dead, you will be saved. So today, I want to give you the opportunity to consider eternity. If you've never received Jesus as your personal Lord and Savior, or if you're unsure if heaven is your final destination, then pray this prayer out loud:

Heavenly Father, in the name of Jesus, I come before you today with my hands lifted high and my heart full of humility. I have made so many mistakes, yet You loved me enough to send Your only Son to die for me. I cannot fathom that kind of love, but nevertheless, You say I am worth it. No man could love me like You, no friend could love me like You, no human being could ever love me like You; it is You who loves me the most. And because of that, I surrender myself to You. Today I am Yours, fully and completely, and through You I will never be the same. Forgive me, transform me, and fill me with Your Spirit. I love You, and thank You for loving me. Amen.

Congratulations. You've just been set free.

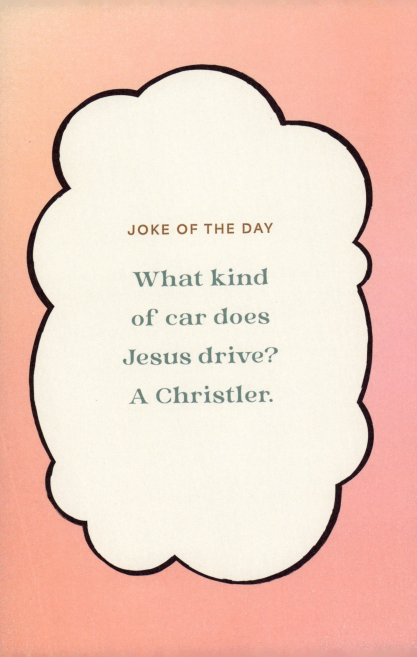

# You Do What We Doubt

*You are the God who performs miracles;*
*You display Your power among the peoples.*

PSALM 77:14

My mom is not only the cutest little southern belle who has ever walked the planet, she is tough as nails. Her hair is usually bouncy with body from hot rollers, her makeup tastefully accentuates her lovely little face, and yet she has no problem manually syphoning my birthing tub water when the pump stopped working (I'll spare you the details, but you can use your imagination as to how gross that was). So when test results revealed she most likely had breast cancer, it didn't intimidate her one bit. I, on the other hand, was devastated.

Doctors requested an immediate biopsy because her numbers of possibility were very high. We had friends with lower numbers who received positive biopsy results, so I was resigned to the fact that Momma was sick. With numbers like hers, of course she was cancer positive. I doubted God. There was no way He could perform a miracle like that; because numbers don't lie, right?

Goodness gracious, oh me of little faith! The call came in a few days later: no trace of breast cancer whatsoever! I couldn't believe it. All I could say was, "Oh praise You,

Father! Praise You, Father! You did this! You are the Healer!"

Thomas, one of Jesus's disciples, dealt with doubt too. Even after seeing Jesus perform miracles time and time again, he didn't believe it when his friends told him Jesus rose from the grave. He basically said, "There ain't no way, bro. Unless I can see the holes in his hands, y'all are tripping." Of course, we know how that story ends. Jesus showed up, and Thomas's reaction was similar to mine.

It's okay to feel doubt, It's just not okay to stay there! Doubt pulls circumstances out of God's hands and into our own. How easily we forget who we're talking about here: this is the God who created the world, who parted the seas, who conquered the grave. This same God loves you so much, He intricately formed you in your mother's womb. Oh friend, don't you know He can do it? The power of God is the same yesterday, today, and forever.

> God, forgive me for doubting You.
> No matter how bleak things seem,
> I believe You can do anything. Amen.

# No Shame in His Name

*Go home to your own people and tell them how much the Lord has done for you, and how He has had mercy on you.*

MARK 5:19

*(Trigger warning: what I'm about to share may be difficult to read. It involves the suffocating emotions that surround the topic of sexual abuse within the church. Be advised.)*

At the age of 17, I went through a breakup. It wrecked me, so my youth pastor suggested I work with him to redirect my mind. After weeks of private one-on-one conversations, his spiritual counsel started to shift. The man who once preached to me about saving myself for marriage started telling me that sex would heal my pain. It was twisted, it was confusing—yet, being the wounded, broken, and naive virgin teenager I was, I listened. After all, why would the man who led me spiritually for years steer me in the wrong direction?

Eventually, the unthinkable happened. He stole my purity. The shame of it still haunts me to this day, even though it took years to realize none of it was my fault.

Twelve years later, I told my husband, and my youth

pastor confirmed it to be true. However, after my husband appropriately contacted their church and school, we were slapped with a defamation lawsuit for nearly a million dollars. My youth pastor and his wife lied about us repeatedly under oath, and the experience was absolutely excruciating. However, I serve a God who always exposes the truth; the courts ruled against my former youth pastor and his wife, and my husband and I were vindicated fully.

Sharing this testimony of God's goodness was tough. But because the Lord rescued me from shame, absolved me from blame, and made me spotless in His name, I knew I must!

Our testimonies are never intended to remain hidden. Webster defines the word "testimony" as a public recounting of a religious conversion or experience— meaning, when God moves mountains in your life, people need to hear about it! It brings healing, it empowers boldness, and it encourages others to live as a vessel for the kingdom of God.

God wants to bring beauty from your ashes.

Whatever your story is, be bold in it, and walk in total victory!

*God, give me the courage to tell others about all good things You've done for me. Amen.*

# Never Early, Never Late

*There is an appointed time for everything.
And there is a time for every
event under heaven.*

ECCLESIASTES 3:1 NASB1995

You probably remember me mentioning that I'm a total psychopath when it comes to being on time. I will rush like a mad woman to get there, lest the humiliation of being two minutes late is too much for me to bear. (I'm working on this; goodness gracious, help me, Jesus.)

When it comes to God's timing for answering our prayers, that feeling of being out of control can grip us. "Why isn't He healing me when I ask? When will I ever get that promotion? Doesn't He realize we're on a time crunch here?"

Jairus, a wealthy and influential religious leader, felt this very emotion. After hearing Jesus was in town, Jairus begged Him to come heal his dying daughter. As they fought through the crowds toward Jairus' home, Jesus suddenly stopped. "Who touched me?" He asked. Jairus, I'm sure, was confused and in disbelief. "Bro, did you not hear me? My daughter is dying!" (A loose interpretation of Jairus's thoughts, of course.)

However, even in such a life-threatening hour where time was of the essence, Jesus had a plan. The woman with the issue of blood touched Him in the crowd, and Jesus healed her right there on the spot. Seeing this, I'm sure, gave Jairus hope. But to his dismay, a messenger reached Jairus with horrible news—his daughter had died. It was too late. Seeing his grief, Jesus turned to Jairus and said, "Don't be afraid, just believe." Because Jairus had just witnessed that miracle in the crowd, he had enough faith to believe this Messiah could restore his daughter's life. And, of course, that's exactly what Jesus did.

The timing of this miracle was significant. If Jesus had healed the woman with the issue of blood any sooner, Jairus wouldn't have seen it. Jesus didn't stop in the crowd because He was delaying time, He did this because it was the perfect time.

Our Lord is never too early, and He is certainly never too late. There is a purpose behind the timing. In the meantime, like Jairus, all we need to do is quit worrying and have faith. Oh friend, won't He do it!

> God, I trust Your timing. Help
> my unbelief and give me peace
> in the waiting. Amen.

# Silly Ol' Sheep

*When Jesus landed and saw
a large crowd, He had compassion
on them, because they were like
sheep without a shepherd. So He
began teaching them many things.*

MARK 6:34

There is a hilarious viral video of a sheep and a shepherd. The sheep is stuck headfirst in a crevasse, in distress, unable to get out, and in dire need of help. The shepherd comes from behind to the rescue the sheep and pulls him out by his hind legs. Feeling jolly and free, the sheep jubilantly starts hopping away. However, he accidentally dives headfirst, again, right back into the same crevasse. If we're being real, sheep are probably the most airheaded animals out of all of God's creatures. Goodness gracious, bless their hearts; they do make comfy clothes, though, so they at least have that going for them.

Because they are (sometimes mindless) followers, sheep are fully dependent on a loving shepherd to lead them in the right direction. And believe it or not (brace yourselves for a cold, hard truth), God made us the exact same way. He purposefully created us in such a way that we will always need a Good Shepherd to lead us on paths of righteousness for His name's sake.

Many in our generation today are trying so hard to do life on their own. However, no matter how hard we try to do it alone, human beings were made for connection. We were made to be in relationship with our Creator. Just as a sheep trusts its shepherd to guide, protect, and provide for it, we must trust God as our Shepherd. He is the one who leads us on the right path, protects us from harm, and provides for our needs. When we try to go it alone, or try to find a shepherd elsewhere, we often find ourselves lost, vulnerable, and lacking the true fulfillment that can only come from our divine connection.

What a relief it is to know we have a Good Shepherd! He adores us so much. Even when we are led astray, He will always come to our rescue.

> God, thank You for leading me.
> I choose to follow You all the
> days of my life. Amen.

# A Heavenly Mantle

*Say a quiet yes to God and*
*He'll be there in no time. Quit dabbling in sin.*
*Purify your inner life. Quit playing the field.*
JAMES 4:8 THE MESSAGE

My mother-in-law is a firecracker of a lady. Despite her itty-bitty stature of five-foot-zilch, her spiky hair and her larger-than-life presence is that of a mighty lion. God has placed a call upon her life that radiates with a holy fire, and goodness gracious, has she embraced it.

However, her calling has not come without its challenges. She has been mocked for her spiritual giftings, mocked for worshipping through dance, and mocked for simply being a woman in ministry. Yet, none of it fazes her. Because her identity is so rooted in Christ, she has never tried to be anyone else, and she has never strayed from acting in obedience to the voice of God.

As someone who married into the family, I've watched her example from the sidelines for over a decade. I've always possessed a quiet honor for her; whether it's watching her pray for someone at a grocery store or dance at a conference in front of many, it is visibly apparent that my mother-in-law allows God to move and flow effortlessly through her.

You and I also have a heavenly mantle placed upon our

lives. God has destined all of us to do great and mighty things for Him. That's why it is so important for us to surrender our lives completely, saturate our hearts with His Word, and seek His wisdom and guidance every step of the way.

There is an enemy who is so intimidated by the power of God inside you that he will do anything to keep you from making a difference. He will lie to you by saying "that's not your calling," or he will convince you to neglect your gifts completely. However, when we ignore our call, it will always lead to a fall; we must fully embrace what God designed us to do!

Maybe as you're reading this, you can picture God's call in the back of your mind. Maybe pain, or fear, has kept you from acting in obedience. But today, walk in lionlike boldness because greater is He who is in you than he who is in the world!

> God, no matter the opposition,
> I choose to fulfill the call You have
> placed upon my life. Amen.

# Just One Praise Away

*Clap your hands, all you nations; shout to God with cries of joy.*

PSALM 47:1

Growing up, my sister was a competitive gymnast. She was good too. Her personality is magnetic, comedic, and leader-like, so naturally, becoming a cheerleader seemed reasonable. And goodness gracious, what a great fit it was for her! She tossed girls into the air like weightless ragdolls, danced with pom-poms and joyful jubilancy, and jumped like a cricket on crack during touchdowns. I, for the most part, was just another maniac in the stands: screaming and clapping and going bonkers alongside sweaty middle-aged dads and painted-bodied frat guys.

People go nuts over their favorite teams and even more nuts when on the verge of a big win. Yet, why do we hesitate to boldly celebrate God when He pulls through for us? Why are we so extroverted with football or soccer or baseball, but when it comes to our worship, we're so reserved?

Having a clearer understanding of who God is and what He has done for us makes all the difference. So often we allow one big fumble to cloud our minds and take precedence over the many victories and mercies of God, myself included. Yet, let me ask you this:

How loud would you praise if you were *one praise away* from a breakthrough?

How loud would you praise if you were *one praise away* from an answered prayer?

How loud would you praise if you were *one praise away* from the healing, restoration, and transformation you've longed for?

Remember who God is today. And worship Him with everything inside of you. Give Him a shout of praise, for the best is yet to come!

> **God, today I shout Your praises! I will be unashamed to lift my hands and worship You, now and forevermore! Amen.**

# Absorbing the Word

*"If anyone has ears to hear, let them hear.
Consider carefully what you hear."*

MARK 4:23-24

"Can we please hurry to the restaurant? We're starving!" our children exclaimed.

"Whoa, before you start talking about your guts, tell me what you learned in Sunday school today!" I said with a twinge of annoyance.

"Um, I don't remember," they mumbled.

"You must have learned something!" I replied, this time with a full-on tone of annoyance. Yet, after taking a deep breath, I asked myself: "Okay, what did *you* learn from the sermon this morning, Hannah?" And goodness gracious, my brain farted. I couldn't remember a thing. Probably because I, too, was hyper-focused on lunch plans. It was a humbling moment, that's for sure.

Truly though, why does this happen? We try to read the Word or listen to an edifying message, yet our attention gets redirected, and we don't absorb things like we should. I can't be the only one, right?

Since Jesus knew our brains were that of a squirrel's, He shared the parable of the sower and the seeds (Mark 4).

Seeds were scattered on a path, but the birds ate them up. How often do we hear the Word, but the enemy uses distraction to hinder the truth from rooting inside of us?

Seeds were scattered on rocky, shallow soil, but the growth was scorched and had no root. How often do we enthusiastically shout our "yes and amens," but when things get tough, we quit living out the Word?

Seeds were scattered among thorns, and when they sprouted, they were choked out. How often do we hear the Word, but our compromising lifestyles choke out the truth?

Finally, some seeds were scattered on good soil, and it produced an entire crop. This happens to us when we hear the Word, receive it, commit to living by it, and fulfill our call in spreading the gospel.

When we truly absorb the Word of God, it takes root, and we flourish in every area of our lives. Before spending quality time with the Lord today, consider this: turn on worship music, close your eyes, quiet your soul, and sit in silence. Allow the presence of God to fill the room. May you become good soil and fully absorb every word He speaks!

> God, I declare today that I am
> a sponge for Your Word. Amen.

# There You Are

*The L<small>ORD</small> your God is in your midst,*
*a mighty one who will save;*
*he will rejoice over you with gladness;*
*he will quiet you by his love;*
*he will exult over you with loud singing.*

ZEPHANIAH 3:17 ESV

I once attended a convention for work. (Side note: am I the only one who gags at the idea of huge crowds and lots of walking and a low mental battery after talking to bunches of peeps? Goodness gracious, help me, Jesus.) However, this trip happened to be extremely pivotal and life-changing, and taught me lessons I still remember to this day.

One of these "gold nuggets" was when one of the speakers said, "When you walk into a room, instead of being a *'here I am'* kind of person, be a *'there you are'* kind of person."

*"There you are"* kind of people exhibit a genuine interest in those around them. They embody humility and meekness in the midst of success, compassion in their interactions with others, and eye contact that is so personal it's as if no one else is in the room. There is something so beautiful about authentically embracing someone else's presence and hearing what they have to say. It brings down defenses, and the interaction leaves an everlasting impact. However, people like this are few and far between. If we can count the

amount of people who truly made us feel seen and heard, it's probably limited to one hand.

Jesus, even in all His majesty and fame and glory, is very much of a *"there you are"* kind of God. When we worship Him, He always finds a way to embrace us with a *"there you are."* When we thank Him, He always finds a way to bless us again with a *"there you are."* And after we make mistakes and humbly walk back into His arms, He always welcomes us home with a *"there you are."*

God isn't forcing us to recognize His majesty with an iron fist. He isn't a celebrity who gets irritated or disinterested with our questions or presence. Instead, He intimately meets us where we are and embraces us like we're the only thing that matters.

> God, thank You for seeing me.
> Help me to be a "there you are"
> kind of person for someone today,
> just as You are with me. Amen.

# A "Word" for the Year

*How much better to get wisdom than gold, to get insight rather than silver!*

PROVERBS 16:16

A common tradition nowadays is to declare a "word" for the new year. Beginning January 1, people choose a "word to live by" that projects their goals and aspirations and sets the tone for the next 365 days. Jokingly, I thought of choosing a word like "nacho" because the devil is "nacho" friend, or "Anita" because I'm a sinner and "Anita" Savior. (Okay, that's enough dad jokes for today. Goodness gracious.)

However, one year, I decided to choose a real word with real intentionality of what I wanted my life to look like. After taking a deep dive into the book of Proverbs and reading about Solomon in the book of I Kings, I picked the word *wisdom*.

Solomon, King David's son who eventually became king himself, asked God for only one thing. He didn't ask for a long life, riches, or vengeance against those who had done him wrong. He simply asked for wisdom, mainly to help him properly handle his new role as an inexperienced king. God granted him this request, and Solomon's supernatural wisdom produced perfect discernment in the decisions he made during his reign. As a result, he was the most successful, trustworthy, wealthy, beloved, and superior king in the history of Israel.

Like Solomon, we are inexperienced people. Some are new to a job, marriage, parenting, or even being a Christian. Having wisdom in every untraveled road of life prevents us from making unnecessary mistakes and allows God to take control in our decision-making. With wisdom, we will choose words and actions that lead to favor. With wisdom, we will know how to navigate sticky situations. With wisdom, we will make decisions that lead to victory over the enemy. Stability in our physical, emotional, mental, relational, and even financial lives comes when wisdom is the principal thing.

What areas of your life need more of God's wisdom? Is there something you're dealing with that you've never walked through before? Are there circumstances that remain unchanged no matter how hard you try? If so, pray for wisdom. Read through Proverbs and I Kings. When you ask God for it, you will receive it!

> God, I want wisdom in every area of my life. Help me to strive for this above all things. Amen.

# A Solution Seeker

*I can do everything through Christ,
who gives me strength.*
PHILIPPIANS 4:13 NLT

My brother has a horse named TJ. Sorry, a dog, not a horse, a dog.

For real though, this 120-plus pound rottweiler is so massive, he genuinely looks like a small horse.

One day, TJ went missing. The back gate was accidentally left open, allowing the perfect opportunity for that massive high-energy mutt to experience temporary freedom. Despite his menacing beast-like looks, TJ is actually a total sweetheart. However, the rest of the world doesn't know that; therefore, our family dreaded the thought of someone irrationally harming him out of "fear" and "self-defense."

Since most of our family lives close to each other, our sister, Payton, sprang into action in the quest to find that runaway rascal. Her thoughts immediately went into solution-mode: "If I were TJ, where would I go?" she asked herself. Within seconds, she remembered how TJ loved to chase ducks; sure enough, in a large water reservoir behind our brother's house, there he was: a hairy black and brown maniac in the distance, splashing around and terrorizing every duck family who lived nearby. TJ was safe, our family was relieved, and

God received the glory for that positive outcome! *Goodness gracious, that silly dog.*

Because we live in a fallen world, dreadful things are bound to happen. We feel pain, grief, fear, anxiety, and a slew of other stinging emotions that come with everyday problems. However, one thing is for sure: there are always solutions to life's pollutions. While so many solutions are found in Scripture, solutions are also discovered when we surrender our problems to God and allow the Holy Spirit to direct us toward the next right step.

Our job is to be a solution seeker, not a problem dweller. Centralizing our attention solely on the negative aspects of something will delay the process of making it right again. God wants us to live joyfully and by faith! Through Him, we experience healing after hard things. Through Him, we experience resolve amid conflict. Through Him, we experience enough strength to conquer every troublesome circumstance.

Today, divert your attention away from the problem and above to the Savior. He will reveal the solution you need, guaranteed!

> God, help me to become solution minded. I desire to experience peace and to walk forward in the right direction. Amen.

**JOKE OF THE DAY**

I'll tell you one miracle that no one talks about from the Bible—and that's the one where Jesus has 12 close friends in His 30's.

# Sticks and Stones

*Do not let any unwholesome talk come out of your mouths, but only what is helpful for building others up according to their needs.*

EPHESIANS 4:29

"Sticks and stones may break my bones, but words will never hurt me," No way, dude! Words hurt! In fact, dare I say that a hurtful word is more painful than a slap in the face, especially if it's said by someone you love?

Unfortunately, in life, people will say things to intentionally hurt us. However, we are also guilty of doing the same to ourselves. How often do we speak things, verbally or subconsciously, that sling sticks and stones at our own hearts? I've been guilty of saying things like "Ew, why is the sound of your voice so cringy?" or "Girl, if your nostrils were a bra size, they'd be a DD." (That one is actually kind of funny, but goodness gracious, that's besides the point.) And worst of all: "You do realize you're a failure, right? God can no longer use a hot mess like you."

Words are an effective tool the enemy uses to steal, kill, and destroy, and no one knows this more than the prophet Elijah. He was lied about, hated on, and viciously attacked by the words of his enemies. Running from execution and overwhelmed with despair, Elijah cried out to God and said, "I have had enough, Lord. Let me die, I am no better than my ancestors" (see I Kings 19:4). Despite what others said about him and what he said about himself, God showed great compassion for Elijah. He sent an angel to feed him and minister to him, and eventually God avenged him from his enemies in a powerful way.

While we can't control what others say about us, we can control every word that comes out of our own mouths. Before speaking, we must proceed with caution. If we are tempted to speak loathsomely about ourselves, or if we are tempted to speak hurtfully about someone else, we must resist; and, hypothetically, put a straitjacket on our crazy pieholes.

God gifted us with communication as a tool for healing. Speaking life will improve how we see ourselves, better our relationships with others, and further our closeness with Christ.

> God, let my words be like honey, and convict me if they don't. Help me speak in a way that only produces life. Amen.

# From Burnout to Balance

*Your faith will be like gold that has been tested in a fire. And these trials will prove that your faith is worth much more than gold that can be destroyed. They will show that you will be given praise and honor and glory when Jesus Christ returns.*
I PETER 1:7 CEV

Burnout is a thing. Our jobs, our families, and our commitments can simultaneously require so much of us that it gets overwhelming. Metaphorically, it's like your clothes are being pulled in so many directions that it leaves you with tangled shoelaces, a ripped-up shirt, a snapped rubber band dangling on matted hair, and an epically massive wedgie. *Goodness gracious, what a visual that was.*

Historically, burnout leaves me feeling disheveled, whiny, and short-fused; and clearly, that's not good. However, after reading I Peter 1:7, the Lord downloaded another perspective about burnout that made me think:

*What if God uses burnout as a subconscious signal to bring balance in certain areas of our lives? What if He allows us to feel burnout so we can recognize that He desires to purify our hearts in one way or another?*

God doesn't want us to burn out; instead, He wants to burn from within us. He desires our spiritual life, our family life, and our professional life to harmonize in equal parts. When it doesn't, He shows up! Look how He did so in the Bible:

When Shadrach, Meshach, and Abednego were thrown into the furnace, the fire didn't consume them; instead, God met them in the flames. They walked out not even smelling like smoke, and they were forever changed.

When Moses saw the burning bush, it didn't wither and reduce to ashes; instead, God revealed His holiness. Moses, too, walked away forever changed.

Just like the flames didn't destroy Shadrach, Meshach, and Abednego or the bush, your burnout won't destroy you. God's refining fire will boost your faith and leave you with a refreshed, purified heart. If the scorch of overwhelm has left you feeling impatient, prideful, or wounded, your heavenly Father is simply signaling your spirit to walk in balance once again. Embrace His loving, purifying process, and be forever changed by His all-consuming fire!

> God, burn away anything in my heart and life that doesn't belong. I desire balance in my life, and I want Your Spirit to light a fire inside of me. Amen.

# For Such a Time as This

*Who knows, perhaps you have come to your royal position for such a time as this.*

ESTHER 4:14 CSB

Whitney has been one of my besties for over twenty years. She's patient, funny, and absolutely darling. We walked through boyfriend breakups together, jammed out to Nickelback together (goodness gracious, don't judge us), became wives and moms together, and now we spend some time every summer together. Looking back, I don't know how I would have navigated those wonky and wild twenty years without her. In fact, if things went according to plan, I wouldn't have.

For an entire decade before she was born, Whitney's parents tried to concieve. It felt impossible. They cried out to God ceaselessly for a baby, but nothing happened. Finally, ten years later, they gave birth to a beautiful little girl, and she was everything they ever prayed for and more.

After knowing this story for years, I realized something. If God had granted them a child any sooner, it wouldn't have been Whitney. If He had answered their prayer right away, her parents wouldn't have known how wonderful she was. If they had conceived ten, seven, or even five years earlier, I wouldn't have had my best friend. God's plan for Whitney's arrival was perfect. He knew that out of every moment in time, she was born for such a time as this.

So often, people express feeling like they were born in the wrong era. And today, there is an underlying fear of bringing children into this world due to how dreadful, dangerous, and dysfunctional it is. However, our world has always been fallen! Every past generation has timestamps of traumatic events that forever shaped the course of humanity. Yet, every single time, God used a group of people (or one person) to courageously step in and put an end to the enemy's schemes. He used Queen Esther during her time, He used Harriet Tubman during her time, He used Mother Theresa during her time, and He will use you during this time.

We are divinely and timely appointed. He handpicked us to live in this time of history for a reason. Rise up with courage! His plan for you, and the generations after you, is good.

> God, I trust You. I know I was born at the right time. Use me, and the children after me, for Your glory. Amen.

# Armor Up, Baby

*Put on the full armor of God,
so that you can take your stand
against the devil's schemes.*

EPHESIANS 6:11

When our daughter Lace was little, she was obsessed with the armor of God. She would wear the whole getup too: a kid-sized plastic version of a helmet, breastplate, sword, belt, shoes, and shield. She'd raise that sword with a stone-cold face, walk around the house valiantly quoting those Scriptures, and even run to "rescue" her brother after hearing him wake up from his nap. It was the most adorable, funny, wholesome thing.

One night, Lace had a bad dream. You could hear the trembling in her voice as she spoke. But when she finished sharing, she cleared her throat and took a deep, courageous breath:

"Mom, I told the devil to go away in Jesus's name, and I told him that I had the armor of God. I wasn't scared after that, so I went back to sleep."

Goodness gracious, my momma heart.

One thing is true: we are in a spiritual battle, every single day. We cannot ignore the fact that we have an enemy. We cannot wish away the fact that the devil is alive and well, seeking to devour at every vulnerable moment. But more than his plans to mess with us, the enemy wants to mess with our kids. It is high time for every parent, aunt, uncle, and mentor to shout "Not today, Satan! You will not touch our children! You will not succeed in putting them in harm's way! You will not mess with their minds, harm their bodies, or thwart the call God has upon their life. We cover our children and command you to *flee* in the *name of Jesus*!"

When we instill God's Word into our hearts, we become dangerous to the enemy. At the spoken name of Jesus, he retreats in terror. The armor of God protects us from sin, trouble, and harm, and weaponizes us in a way that terrifies that little loser, Satan.

It's time to armor up, baby! Spiritually equip yourselves and lead your children as mighty warriors for the kingdom of God!

> God, I know that with Christ, I am a threat to the enemy. I will put on the full armor and stand firm in the face of every spiritual battle. Amen.

# P.U.S.H.

*The suffering won't last forever. It won't be long before this generous God who has great plans for us in Christ—eternal and glorious plans they are!—will have you put together and on your feet for good.*

I PETER 5:10 THE MESSAGE

I had no idea what I was signing up for. I decided to have our first baby at a birth center—and totally unmedicated. After watching a documentary called *The Business of Being Born* and seeing their beautiful birth stories (with minimal moans and groans, mind you) I thought, "Oh yeah. I can do that."

Goodness gracious, bless my little heart.

My water broke, the contractions started, and we got in the car. However, 5 p.m. traffic in the Dallas/Fort Worth metroplex will always leave you at a standstill. Not to mention, we were running out of gas, so we had no choice but to fill up. If you can only imagine the sounds of my guttural animalistic noises as my husband stood at Exxon, pump in hand. I'm sure I traumatized the kids in the adjacent car while they blankly stared with Gatorade in one hand and M&M's in the other.

Even though I undoubtedly caused hearing damage for the people in our car, we eventually reached the birth center. My precious midwife sprang into action, looked at me with a serious face and a stern tone, and said: "Hannah, it's time to push, right now."

Finally, surrounded by our entire family, Lace Avery Crews was born. She was healthy, beautiful, and perfect; the euphoria of holding her in my arms instantly made me forget the intensity it took to get her here.

Like birth, there are times in life where things are wildly intense. The labor it takes to survive heartache, suffering, grief, and pain can be overwhelming. Yet as it says in I Peter, our suffering won't last forever! Since God has great plans for us, He will put the broken pieces of our hearts back together and help us back to our feet for good. In the meantime, we are to P.U.S.H., which stands for:

Pray
Until
Something
Happens

You are soon to experience the beautiful result of God's mercy and grace, my friend. Until then, P.U.S.H.—your redemption is on its way!

> God, give me the strength to P.U.S.H.
> I will stand firm in Your promises to
> redeem every pain of my past. Amen.

# Please Like Me

*Just as the Father has loved Me,
I have also loved you;
abide in My love.*
JOHN 15:9 NASB1995

Let's lay out a scenario. Have you ever had a chance to hang with someone you admire, and wanted so badly for them to like you? You pre-record the conversation in your head and develop expectations of how you should speak or act around them. Then, when you finally talk to them, you're only trying to think of the wittiest, most insightful, or most charming response. Afterward, you feel like a nincompoop because you said something weird and wish you weren't so awkward. And when it's all said and done, it hits you: you realize that you were so self-preoccupied that you only cared about appearing cool to that person, rather than caring about the actual person?

That's a lot, I know. Goodness gracious, I hope it doesn't sound too cuckoo. But I think all of us can agree that at some point in our lives, we wanted so badly to be loved that we compromised who we were in order to gain acceptance. Believe it or not, this isn't just high school immaturity we're referring to here. This happens at job interviews, at celebrity meet-and-greets, with new mom-friends at the park, or even in the dating scene. The desire to be loved and wanted is so innate. But how often we forget that we have been loved and wanted all along!

Seeking approval from God is more important than seeking approval from others, and finding that approval from God always leads to finding approval from others. A relationship with God refines our character, and it allows us to make a greater impact in the lives of those around us. And God already thinks we are lovable, despite our flaws and quirks and insecurities.

You are already loved. You are already wanted. And He is in constant pursuit of you, wooing you close to love Him in return!

*God, thank You for loving me, and liking me, even when I don't see myself that way. I long to give more of myself to You and to find approval from You in every area of my life. Amen.*

# Unlimited Creativity

*The Lord is the everlasting God,
the Creator of the ends of the earth.
He will not grow tired or weary, and His
understanding no one can fathom.*

ISAIAH 40:28

My ministry involves a lot of brainstorming. Sometimes it involves producing funny videos with faith-based humor; sometimes it involves writing redonkulous devotions like this (Thanks for hanging in there so far. Goodness gracious, you're kind). But for the most part, the process of creating can sometimes be extremely draining. You run into dead ends and draw blanks, and any creative juices you had seemed to have been sucked out like a pouch of Capri Sun. Other times, seeing someone else's creativity leaves you feeling like yours is peanuts, or that you're just not creative to begin with. However, that's a bunch of bologna! You have no idea how innovative, prolific, and original you truly are! Let me tell you why.

When we think of the word "creator," we immediately think of God. He is the Creator of the heavens, the earth, and every form of life. He is constantly in the process of making something new, and His creativity has no limits in any way, shape, or form.

Here's the cool part: since we have been chosen by the Creator, and since we were created in His image, God has given us all an individual (and highly unique) form of creativity. Believe it or not, there is an unlimited amount of creativity that runs through your veins. You might love creating community among your peers, creating beautiful spaces in your home, creating an atmosphere of joy, or creating new concepts that inspire those around you. Whatever it is, the gift of creativity is crowned upon your head.

A prayer I often pray is "Father, speak to me in a dream. Give me ideas as I sleep that can only come from You." I cannot tell you how often He delivers, and it boosts my faith every time! Through you, God intends to use your gifts and abilities as a tool to glorify Him and capture the hearts of the lost. He is always doing a new thing, and His creativity within you has no limits!

*God, thank You for always coming up with creative ways to pursue my heart. Help me to operate in my creative gifts, and use me for Your glory. Amen.*

# Satan: The Ultimate Copycat

> "And no wonder, for even Satan disguises himself as an angel of light."
>
> II CORINTHIANS 11:14 ESV

Oscar Wilde said, "Imitation is the sincerest form of flattery." However, if I can be completely transparent with you, imitation used to be a previous (and completely juvenile) pet peeve of mine. I don't know if it's the artist in me or if it's just a super stubborn desire to be different, but copycat-like-scenarios used to drive me so far up the wall I'd have to pause for a deep breath, say a "let it go" prayer, and eat a couple of Oreos with some ice-cold milk. *Goodness gracious, the drama. I've grown in grace since then, I promise.*

Speaking of imitators, the devil is the biggest copycat of all time. He isn't original, at all, and he never comes up with anything new. He tries so hard to piggyback off God and uses deception to lead people astray. For example, in Exodus, Pharaoh instructed Moses and Aaron to perform a sign from God. Aaron threw down his staff, and it turned into a serpent. Pharaoh then instructed his own sorcerers to imitate it, which they did with magic and evil arts. However, Aaron's staff immediately swallowed up the sorcerers' staffs, making fools out of them and proving that the devil is just a big fat copycat who will never overcome our God.

In our case, Satan tries so hard to tempt us with the same things. He'll reintroduce the same vices we struggle with, disturb our sleep with the same nightmares, and repeat the same lies that steal our joy. And, even more obviously, he is trying so hard to deceive us into believing that evil things are good, and good things are evil.

We must no longer give the enemy any credit for things that are not his! As children of the Most High, we have the authority to rebuke every plot against our lives and say, "Get thee behind me, Satan!" Recognize when he tries to copy the same tactics and imitate the same lies. Pause, take a deep breath, and take authority through prayer. And if you'd like, eat an Oreo while you're at it.

> Lord, thank You for the comfort of knowing that You have overcome the world. The enemy has been defeated, and I will lift my voice in victory. Amen.

# Good Fruit, Good Impact

*"You did not choose me, but I chose you. I appointed you to go and produce fruit and that your fruit should remain, so that whatever you ask the Father in My name, He will give you."*
JOHN 15:16 CSB

One time I did a Q&A session in my Instagram stories, opening it up to anything people wanted to chat about. One person asked my opinion on how to deal with a difficult coworker they were forced to be around. I thought, dang, what a great question, because, *goodness gracious*, people can be total toots; and, sometimes, we have no choice but to spend time with individuals who aren't our fave. It could be a personality clash or past hurts, or maybe they just have really stinky B.O.

I responded with something like, "Be kind, have boundaries, don't take offense if they act like a donkey." But, from experience, I know that is way easier said than done. I later reflected on my answer, and even though what I said wasn't entirely incorrect, I wanted to know what Scripture said.

The Lord directed me to Galatians, where it talks about the fruit of the Spirit. These character traits are ones we need to always exude: love, joy, peace, patience, kindness, goodness, faithfulness, gentleness, and self-control.

However, other Bible translations refer to the fruit of patience as *longsuffering*. When I looked up the definition, longsuffering means to "have or show patience in spite of trouble, especially those caused by other people." Reading this hit me like a ton of bricks and enhanced my outlook dramatically.

When we showcase a longsuffering attitude around difficult people, they experience healing through grace. Having patience with others cloaks us with honor and exemplifies a loving example of Christ. Showing good fruit is life-giving and sweet; when we do this even around tough people, it allows God to move behind the scenes in their lives, and ours.

Believe it or not, God loves those difficult folks just as much as He loves us. When we choose to see others the way Jesus does, it brings blessing and makes His heart leap! In any triggering moment, remember longsuffering, and ask God to clothe you with it.

> God, help me with longsuffering today.
> You love the difficult people I'm around
> just as much as You love me; let my
> spirit showcase Your patience. Amen.

# Girl, Receive That Compliment!

*Gracious words are like a honeycomb,
sweetness to the soul and health to the body.*
PROVERBS 16:24 ESV

I used to be awful at receiving compliments during a conversation. It would make me want to run and hide. And if these compliments were said around others, I'd experience borderline anxiety. After years of this pattern, I started asking myself, "Why do I do this? Why do I start pit-sweating and always redirect the conversation back to the other person's good qualities?"

I soon realized it was fear, and I retraced that fear back to its roots. There were times when a public compliment was sent my way, but counteracting comments would spew out of others who struggled with resentment or insecurity. Other times, someone would speak an overly kind compliment, but I couldn't receive it because I didn't see myself that way. This led me to deflect and redirect every compliment into a conversation that highlighted the complimenter rather than myself.

I did this for years—until one day, my mother-in-law provided me with a different perspective. "When someone compliments you, receiving it with a 'thank you' is like receiving a gift. It makes that person feel like they added something to your life." What a powerful insight! I had no idea that my responses, more than likely, caused a deflated feeling within the individual who was simply trying to pour out a blessing.

While receiving a compliment deposits life inside of you, fully receiving it with a grateful heart boomerangs a supernatural reward back to the one who spoke it. When we drop-kick someone's compliment just because we're afraid of how others will take it or because we don't believe it to be true, it puts a wall up that blocks God from fully operating out of blessing and healing. I challenge you today: receive every word of life spoken over you. And if the opportunity arises, find someone else to compliment and deposit life into their spirit. Kind words heal, lift, and restore—both when we give and receive them.

*"Compliments are tiny gifts that someone bought especially for you. Deflecting their compliment is the same as rejecting their love for you."*
–Eva DeVirgilis

**God, help me take compliments joyfully and fully. I pray I give, and receive, every word of life that is spoken. Amen.**

JOKE OF THE DAY

If Eve risked humanity for an apple, what would she do for a Klondike bar?

# Jesus Is My Homeboy

*Friends come and friends go, but a true friend sticks by you like family.*
PROVERBS 18:24 THE MESSAGE

As a preteen, one of my favorite stores in the mall was Journey. There, I would buy like fourteen different pair of Converse shoes in various colors and patterns. I'd also repeatedly ask my mom for a "Jesus is my Homeboy" T-shirt, which she never bought because she assumed it was blasphemy. I even remember asking her, "But, Mom, homeboy means friend, right?" And I think she responded with something like, "I don't know, it's just slang, and homeboy is a pitiful word to describe Jesus. Like, hello, He's our Savior!" Goodness gracious, it's so funny to me when I think back on that.

Who knows, there might be some truth to what she said, but it made me think about what true friendship really means. From what I've read in books and articles, friendship is defined in these ways:

A preference that two people have for one another.
A desire for regular contact with another person.
A state of mutual trust, support, respect, and admiration.
When another person is useful to you.
When someone's company brings you pleasure.

The life of Jesus shows us that He went through it all when it comes to friendships. Most of His friends followed Him, loved Him, and protected Him, but some betrayed Him, denied Him, and crucified Him. He even had to set boundaries with acquaintances who desired to be His disciples. Even though Jesus still loved them, He knew their motives weren't pure and the friendship wouldn't produce good fruit.

Whether you're struggling in your friend group or if you're longing to find true quality friends, the first step is this: follow Jesus with a pure heart and allow Him to cultivate goodness through you. When you delight in having Jesus as your primary friend, it causes you to be a magnet for friends who show kindness and goodness within their own lives too.

Regardless of your situation, take some time today to focus on having Jesus as your number one homeboy. Pursuing His heart will allow Him to shine through you and positively impact everyone you meet.

> God, I want good friends, and I want to be a good one too. But most importantly, I want a friendship with You. Amen.

# The Type of Comparison No One Talks About

*Do nothing from selfish ambition or conceit, but in humility count others more significant than yourselves.*

**PHILIPPIANS 2:3 ESV**

I'll never forget this day in seventh grade. Our teacher was reading a devotion about comparison. The last sentence she read was something along the lines of, "Therefore, if you find yourself not making as good of grades as someone else, lift your eyes to Jesus and praise Him for the many blessings you have. Or, if you find yourself making better grades than most, bow your head in humility, ask God for a heart of purity, and strive to be an encouragement to others."

Being an immature little clown who happened to make good grades, I decided to bow my head with a cartoon-like facial expression and a double-chinned grin, mainly with the intention of making my friends laugh. But right when I did that, my teacher's eyeballs locked with mine. She raised her brow with a serious look and said,

"What comes after pride, class?"

"A fall!" everyone responded in unison.

Goodness gracious, was I mortified. Even though I wasn't

trying to be prideful, that moment still taught me a powerful lesson. And quite honestly, it instilled a healthy fear of God in me that still remains to this day.

There are two types of comparison. The one most commonly discussed is the type that leaves you feeling insecure, or not as good as someone else. However, there is a form of comparison that isn't talked about nearly enough; and that's the one that leaves you feeling haughty or superior. This is the most dangerous form of comparison and is a stench to the nostrils of God. Be aware of your heart and rebuke this temptation when it arises. Comparison-induced pride will always lead to humbling consequences and will hinder the blessings of God. Both forms of comparison are thieves of joy; therefore, comparison and joy simply cannot coexist. To live a life of joy, we must choose to see others through the eyes of Jesus rather than through the eyes of insecurity or pride.

*Lord, create in me a clean heart. Help me see others the way You do. Strip me from any signs of haughtiness or pride, and show me how to be more like You. Amen.*

# Behind the Scenes

*My Father is always working,
and so am I.*
JOHN 5:17 NLT

Don't let the smiles fool you, family portraits are never what they appear to be. For us, one photoshoot resulted in an embarrassing, uncooperative, screamy, tear-filled day from the bowels of hades. (That may be a little dramatic, but goodness gracious, it was bad.)

Both of our kids whined to go play, flailed and flopped when we said no, screamed when they were asked to smile, and smeared slimy boogers all over their crisp white outfits. My husband made stressed-out-dad comments like "best kids ever" and "yeah, great idea, Hannah, let's reward their terrible behavior with a lollipop." I finally broke down in an adolescent pity party and tearfully cried, "All I wanted was a dad-gum Christmas picture!"

Looking back on that day, I was so clouded by stress and embarrassment that I overlooked the sweetness behind the scenes. My sister goofy-danced behind the photographer to get the kids' attention. My mom gently wiped their noses before each photo and prayed peace over everyone under her breath. The photographer reassured me graciously saying, "I will give you a beautiful family portrait, I promise." And my husband's friend, in the middle of my tearful breakdown in the kitchen, said comfortingly, "Being a mom is the hardest job in the world. You're doing great."

God is always doing little miracles behind the scenes, and His Word proves it. When the people of Israel were enslaved by the Egyptians, God worked behind the scenes to bring a deliverer through Moses. When Joseph was left for dead by his brothers and sold into slavery, God worked behind the scenes to make him an influential leader who forgivingly saved his bloodline. And when Jesus walked the earth, God worked behind the scenes to make a way for us to spend eternity with Him.

Any time circumstances in your life seem too desperate and too broken, God is still working behind the scenes for your good. Even in the mess, even in the stress, even in the grumpiness and irritability—your situation is never too far gone. Eventually, you will see a beautiful portrait of your testimony on display that showcases the goodness and graciousness of God.

God, I know You're always working behind the scenes. Help me to notice little miracles even in the midst of hard days. Amen.

# From In-Law to In-Love

*For where you go, I will go,
and where you lodge, I will lodge.
Your people shall be my people,
and your God, my God.*

RUTH 1:16 NASB1995

I've said this before, but y'all, my mother-in-law (Janet) is a firecracker! We couldn't have more opposite personalities if we tried. As it is with most marriages, adjusting to a new family can be challenging, and goodness gracious, it sure was. But over time, our love for each other grew to such a place that we weren't just in-laws, we were really good friends.

One day, we decided to go on a run through her neighborhood. It was hot, it was humid, and I remember sweating in ungodly places that I didn't realize had sweat glands. As we paced in step together, she stopped for a break and said, "Darlin', feel free to run on ahead of me and get yourself a good workout." Without hesitation, words spilled out of my mouth that could have only come from God. "Listen, Meme," I said, "you're my Naomi. Ruth didn't leave her mother-in-law, and neither will I." Even though I meant it, my words shocked me—it truly was a Holy Spirit inspired statement. We laughed in wonder, embraced in a salty sweaty hug, and continued our run.

The story of Ruth and Naomi is a phenomenal example of the beauty of not only in-law relationships, but also the beauty of women who support each other through the challenges of life. Naomi's husband passed away, and eventually so did her son, Ruth's husband. Even though Naomi begged Ruth to stay behind and remarry, Ruth refused to listen. She was devoted to stay by her mother-in-law's side, and because of that, God brought great favor upon their lives.

As did Ruth and Naomi, Janet and I went from in-law to in-love. And even if it's not an in-law relationship, supporting women with different backgrounds than you, different personalities than you, and different ways of living than you is so important. Ultimately, we are all women loved equally by God with a unique calling upon our lives. Championing each other through the hard seasons of life and running in step with one another results in unstoppable favor and a powerful unity that can only come from Christ.

> God, help me to run lovingly in step with my sisters in Christ. Amen.

# "God, I Want Her Mermaid Fin."

*A heart at peace gives life to the body, but envy rots the bones.*

PROVERBS 14:30

When I was a little girl, I had a favorite pillow. It was a cutout of Ariel from *The Little Mermaid*, vibrant in color and flat from sleeping on it so much. I wanted her cherry red hair, and often asked my mom for a seashell bikini top even though the answer was always no. However, one thing Ariel had that I coveted more than anything was her spectacular fluorescent mermaid tail. I truly believed if I prayed super hard and slept on that Ariel pillow, it would activate some sort of sparkly magic and I'd wake up with a straight-up fin, like, for real.

Of course, that never happened. And I remember asking God, "Why can't I have what she has?"

Don't worry, I'm fully aware now that wanting a mermaid tail was dumb. I mean, goodness gracious, I would've been hopping and flopping around everywhere for the rest of my life. But it made me think: how often have we looked at someone else's life and asked God, "Why can't I have what she has?"

People normally associate those feelings with the term *jealousy*, but actually, that's incorrect. Jealousy is a reaction to the threat of losing something you already have, while envy is an ungodly covetousness for things you don't have. Jealousy in the Bible has a holy connotation and even describes the character of God. However, the Bible considers envy as so destructive, it was written on the Ten Commandments. If entertained long enough, envy will inflame self-centeredness and self-pity. Not to mention, envy is a bitterness producer, which can negatively affect and infect every aspect of one's life.

I know, that got heavy. But let me tell you something: laying all feelings of envy down at the feet of Jesus will allow joy to step in its place. God intended for you to be *you*. He's given you gifts no one else has, and there is no one more capable of fulfilling your unique calling than you. You are His, and you are special. Embrace this truth today!

> God, remove any trace of envy within my heart. I no longer want it to corrode my joy. I am at peace with what I have, and I give You praise for what's to come. Amen.

# Going Backward to Move Forward

*The LORD our God said to us in Horeb,
"You have stayed long enough at this mountain."*

DEUTERONOMY 1:6

For most of us normal people, parallel parking is the most frustrating activity in all humankind. Goodness gracious, I cannot count the amount of attempts it takes me to shimmy my way into one of those spaces sometimes.

One day, after successfully parallel parking in a spot downtown, I returned to my vehicle expecting to drive away with ease. However, a massive truck had backed up so close to my front bumper, it nearly kissed it.

There was no way to drive forward without going backward—which I did, time and time and time again. People were staring, horns were honking, and it was mortifying. Eventually, I went backward enough times to angle my front bumper away from the truck and finally drive forward. What an embarrassing mess, but it's fine, I'll never see those people again. *Hopefully.*

There may be areas of your life where you feel stuck between a rock and a hard place, and no matter how hard you try, it feels like you can't move forward. I've been there. It's frustrating and painful and hopeless all at the same time. However, refusing to move forward from the pain of our past breeds self-pity and keeps us trapped. Thoughts of "woe is me" start to creep in; yet it doesn't change our circumstances one lick, nor does it change the hearts of those around us. Self-pity drains energy, steals joy, and dismantles hope. As Joyce Meyer says, "We can live pitiful, or powerful, but not both."

As painful as it can be, sometimes going backward is the only way to move forward. Sometimes we need to face our past, acknowledge that it happened, and move forward in peace. Other times, expressing sorrow for our mistakes will help us move forward in relationships. And other times, seeking help through a professional counselor will allow us to mend old wounds and receive the supernatural healing Christ paid for on the cross.

Life is lived forward, but it is only understood backward. It may take a few attempts to break free, but once we do, we will finally experience a forward-moving life.

> God, I don't want to remain wounded by my past. Help me acknowledge it with strength and move forward with peace. Amen.

# Fear Is Not Yours to Carry

*The L*ORD *will fight for you;*
*you need only to be still.*

**EXODUS 14:14**

When I was a kid, my cousins convinced me to watch the shark movie *Jaws*, and goodness gracious, my innocent little eyeballs had never seen something so action-packed. Even though the special effects are hilariously fake, getting eaten by a shark quickly moved to the top of my fears list. For years, I struggled with swimming in any body of water where I couldn't see the bottom. Whether it was at a beach or in a lake with zero sharks, images of an open-mouthed great white coming to devour me from the depths haunted my thoughts to the max.

We all have something in our lives that scares the snot out of us. And many times, our minds get clouded with anxiety over hypothetical scenarios that are either unrealistic or out of our control. However, the number one thief of a meaningful life is the presence of anxiety and worry. When we allow anxiety to rule us, it steals our joy, compromises our quality of life, and confines our freedom. Worrying about things doesn't take away tomorrow's troubles, it takes away today's peace.

The enemy uses anxiety and worry as crippling tools.

But what the enemy means for evil, God will use for good; therefore, let's consider anxiety as a spotlight that clearly identifies the things we refuse to surrender. Releasing your worries and anxieties is the ultimate act of trust in the God who loves you—and His perfect love casts out fear. It's important to confidently trust God every single day of the year.

Write down everything that makes you feel anxiety or fear today. Close your eyes in silence, and picture yourself white-knuckling these fears in your hands. Now, relax your fingers one by one, until your hands are fully open. Watch as those fears gently float from your hands, into the merciful and all-powerful hands of Jesus.

Fear is not yours to carry. It's His! Let go and let God.

> God, help me let go of all things that consume me with anxiety, worry, and fear. I desire to cast every care upon You freely so that I can live a life of peace. Amen.

# He Sees the Big Picture

*For whenever our heart condemns us,
God is greater than our heart,
and he knows everything.*

1 JOHN 3:20 ESV

When my sister started dating her husband, I immediately knew it was a perfect match. However, he didn't realize that as a little girl, she would slap me square in the eye socket if I ever tried to cuddle with her. So when I realized this gentle giant found my sister as irresistibly cuddly as I did, I said a prayer for him: "Lord, bless his soul, and protect his face." *Kidding, but not really.*

They finally got engaged, and their original desire was to simply elope. But, as it often does, the wedding plans changed, and they agreed to be married in the mountains of Colorado surrounded by family and friends. The invitations were sent, the dress was purchased, the vendors were booked, and everything appeared to be smooth sailing.

But, a couple of days before their March 20, 2020, wedding day, the entire world shut down. Goodness gracious, "devastating" is an understatement as to how we all felt. While Covid would come to ruin and destroy so much more than my sister's wedding, it was still very hard to see the disappointment on her face. What was supposed to be the most magical day of her life, tragically cancelled. But as it turns out, God was able to use this situation to bring about some very cool circumstances:

The baker donated the wedding cakes to a nursing home full of quarantined elderly who were unable to love on their families.

The wedding coordinator donated all the flowers to a local hospital hosting a "Thank You Luncheon" for weary and overworked healthcare professionals.

My sister and brother-in-law ended up eloping anyway in a private ceremony led by one of our childhood best friends, and her workplace hired a last-minute professional photographer for the occasion.

Initially, it felt like their wedding day dreams were robbed from them; however, God used that unfortunate circumstance to bless hundreds of people, and He granted them the desires of their hearts to be married intimately with no one else around.

The cool thing about God is He has an aerial view of time. His eyes can span across our past, present, and future; therefore, He always knows what is best for us. He sees the big picture. And trust me, the masterpiece He is painting of your life will be more beautiful and meaningful than you can ever imagine!

> God, You see the big picture. May Your will be done in my life, always. Amen.

# You're Cordially Uninvited

*"I have loved you with an everlasting love;
I have drawn you with unfailing kindness."*

JEREMIAH 31:3

I never partied in high school. But when I'd found out there was another rager over the weekend that *no one* invited me to, *again*, it would always sting my little sixteen-year-old soul. A popular reason my classmates would give me is, "Well, you don't drink or anything, so why invite you?" They didn't say it hatefully, but I *hated* hearing that. I'd tell myself things like "Quit being a wimp and just try a stinkin' beer," or "If only I had their parents instead of my strict old fuddy-duddies." Goodness gracious, there were so many times where I was tempted to compromise just so I'd be included by my peers.

After graduating high school, I met up with one of my "partier" friends who lived nearby. As we drove around our hometown reflecting on the last four years, he suddenly told me, "You know, honestly, I thought it was cool that you didn't party with us. We respected you for it." His words made every past feeling of rejection vanish in an instant.

Feeling uninvited, unaccepted, or "not cool enough" always sucks. And in life, there are going to be times where we are purposefully left out due to an unalignment of lifestyles or clash in personalities. Yes, it stings, because as human beings, all we want is to be embraced and loved for who we are. But scenarios like this are intended to draw us closer to our ultimate source of comfort, Jesus. When we focus on a relationship with the God who loves us, it rubs off on us, and we learn to love others the same way, even those who leave us out. God's love takes us on a journey to finding the right person, or people, who will love us back.

Seek a friendship with God. He wants to bless you with girlfriends who pray for you behind your back, a spouse who loves you for your heart more than your body, and a community who flourishes when you're around. On days where you feel cordially uninvited, simply lift your eyes and gaze upon the One who desires your company the most.

> God, with You, I'm always included.
> I'm okay with being uninvited if it is
> not Your perfect will for me. Amen.

# The Most Important Devotion You'll Ever Read (Again)

*"I am the way, the truth, and the life. No one comes to the Father except through Me."*
JOHN 14:6 CSB

If you've been following along, reading one devotion a day, then you just hit the two-month mark! That's dedication. I bet you also floss your teeth every day, don't you? Yep, I knew it. You're a winner.

Awhile back, we talked about the importance of receiving Jesus as your personal Lord and Savior. The amazing thing about God is He will never stop chasing after you, and He will never stop pursuing your heart. However, God is not a puppeteer. He will never force you to love Him back, force you to believe in Him, or force you to accept Him. But His grace will keep knocking on your door anyway, over and over, until your very last breath. If that's not the purest form of love, I don't know what is!

A life with Jesus is much sweeter than one without Him, and a life serving Him is much sweeter than one running from Him. Regardless, life is still hard—but in heaven, the Word of God says that tears, pain, and death are no more.

Choosing Jesus is the most important decision you'll ever make. If you've never received Him as your personal

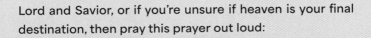

Lord and Savior, or if you're unsure if heaven is your final destination, then pray this prayer out loud:

> Dear God, I am done running from You. I have made so many mistakes, yet You loved me enough to send Your only Son to die for me. I cannot fathom that kind of love, but nevertheless, You say I am worth it. You picked me at my worst, chose me at my ugliest, and embraced me at my lowest. Therefore, I surrender to You. I believe Jesus died for me and rose again. I choose to be Yours, fully and completely, and through You I will never be the same. Forgive me, transform me, and fill me with Your Spirit. I love You, Lord, and thank You for loving me. Amen.

Praise God. May your life be a testament of His goodness and grace, today and forevermore!

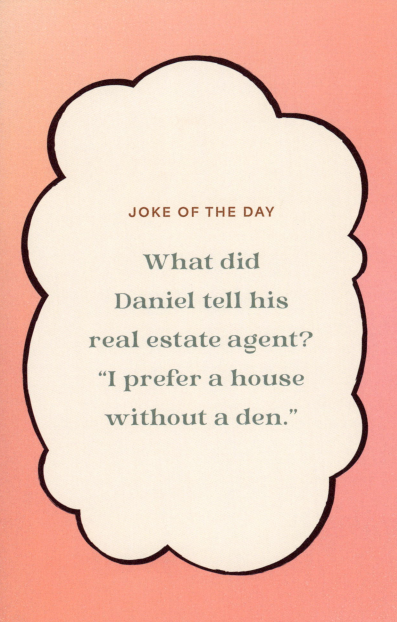

# Make Me a Vessel

*For we are co-workers in God's service;
you are God's field, God's building.*
I CORINTHIANS 3:9

My news director once assigned me a story that was way over my head. It was a topic that was numerical and confusing, like taxes or something. I don't even remember, that's how little it piqued my interest. I begged her to reassign me with something else, because goodness gracious, this blondie has a hard enough time changing a lightbulb let alone interpreting legal documents with a bunch of stupid numbers.

However, my boss didn't budge. She told me to suck it up and do the story. And out of all the stories I did while working at that station, that dumb story was the most watched and most commented on by the viewers. Not only that, I learned a lot about that topic and grew from the challenge. Clearly whatever I learned didn't stick, bless my heart, but still. It was a good lesson at the time!

My job as a reporter was to be a vessel for the station and to pour out information for the benefit of the audience. And as Christians, our job is to be vessels for the Lord and to pour out His Spirit for the benefit of others.

However, being God's vessel and allowing Him to call the shots without input, arguing, or distrust goes against everything engrained within us. At times, it seems easier to be our own boss, question everything, and trust our own instincts; and while those things can be valuable in the natural, God calls us to do the opposite in our spiritual walk with Christ. In order to be a vessel that is functional, practical, and useful for the souls around us, we must allow Him to take the reins over every area of our lives.

We are spiritually eternal beings living through a temporary physical experience. When we fully understand this, it humbles us and allows us to loosen our choke hold of control on life. Giving God all that we are and trusting His assignments allows our vessel to overflow for His glory in ways that we could never do on our own.

*God, make me a vessel. Help me to release the reins of control. I trust that Your plan for my life is more beneficial than mine; humble me, use me, fill me. Amen.*

# Don't Compete, Complete!

*So then let us pursue what makes for peace and for mutual upbuilding.*
ROMANS 14:19 ESV

Friendships with women can be tricky. It is a common stigma that most women are inherently backbiting, envious, and mean. (Not all women, I know! But goodness gracious, have you seen any episodes of *Real Housewives*?) I encountered enough catty little queens growing up that it made me very discerning early on. I could identify which girls felt trustworthy and which girls felt shady—leaving me reserved, careful, and meticulous with whom I spent my time.

Then along came Alison, who I met on the cheer squad in college. And boy oh boy, if I was the envious type, she would have been the perfect target. That girl had more intelligence, more success, more culture, and more popularity in her pinky finger than I had in my entire body combined. Ali was altogether perfect, but her heart of gold made me gravitate to her like a magnet. If I struggled in a routine, she selflessly worked with me after practice. If she was emotionally troubled during a game, I'd crack a joke to lift her spirits. When one of us was in need, the other filled it. It didn't matter that we were in the same school, around the same friends, or involved in the same activities. We made each other better, and we still champion each other to this day.

Competition pushes people to improve in every way: personally, physically, and professionally. But when a competitive spirit leans into pride, tension, and insecurity, it becomes destructive. If the goal is to "show up" someone else or to make them feel inferior, that obsession will lead to loneliness.

We are called to work in harmony with the women around us. God's desire for women is to pray for one another, lift each other up, and live in peace. When our hearts are pure and fully surrendered to Jesus, we can be a good friend to others due to His example.

If you have strengths, pour those strengths into the lives of the women around you. Serve them unconditionally and encourage them ceaselessly; and if you see a need, fill it. We're all in this together!

> God, help us as women to complete each other, not compete with each other. Amen.

# The Pursuit of Peace

*"Peace I leave with you; my peace I give to you. Not as the world gives do I give to you. Let not your hearts be troubled, neither let them be afraid."*

JOHN 14:27 ESV

Throughout her life, my great-aunt Ann had such a peaceful persona about her. Her character was that of a true angel, seemingly never committing any wrongdoing and never exemplifying an ounce of fear. However, her life and circumstances were far from perfect. We watched her experience cancer, a dysfunctional family, being ripped off in business, and taken advantage of for insane amounts of money—simultaneously! That kind of stress would drive any normal human being into complete despair. But Ann wasn't normal.

I remember my mom exasperatingly pleading with her, "Ann! Don't you see everything that is happening?! Don't you understand what is going on in your body and what these low-life losers have done to rob you?" Ann just listened patiently, sat in her recliner, and shrugged her shoulders, "Well, praise the Lord!" she softly said. It made me chuckle, because the circumstances were so insane yet her reaction was so cute. Goodness gracious, nothing moved her. She always knew God had everything under control, and since that was enough for her, Ann lived in peace.

Living in peace does not mean there is an absence of conflict. Rather, peace is when we choose to embody harmony and tranquility in our hearts and minds despite all circumstances. I know that is easier said than done. However, perfect love casts out fear. When we fully understand how much we are loved by God, we can be confident that He has everything under control. And even when things seem out of control, it doesn't matter; knowing who He is allows peace to become second nature.

Peace brings an overwhelming amount of patience, understanding, and compassion. It also clothes us with dignity and strength, where we can still experience joy and laugh without any fear of the future.

God wants to free you from unhealthy fears. He wants to strip you from forming your identity around the bad things that have happened to you. Fully embrace His love; when you do, it will cast out all fear!

> God, give me peace today. I refuse to get worked up today over things I can't control. I choose to trust You joyfully. Amen.

# A Way of Escape

*God is faithful, and he will not let you be tempted beyond your ability, but with the temptation he will also provide the way of escape, that you may be able to endure it.*

I CORINTHIANS 10:13 ESV

In college, there was this guy on the football team. He was older, a Christian, had a brother in the NFL, and was on track to do the same. I really wanted him to notice me, and finally, one day, he did. He asked me out, and I legit almost peed my pants. I told my best friends, started looking at wedding dresses, began to envision baby names, all the things. (Goodness gracious, desperate much?)

The next night, I rushed back to my dorm after class and started getting ready. Just as I was finishing my makeup (which looked bomb by the way, I made sure of it), my phone dinged. It was a text from him, saying, "Hey, I think I'm just gonna bro it out with my dudes tonight." I couldn't believe what I was reading. Like, cancel on me ten minutes before and for a reason *that insulting*? What a tool.

I called my mom in tears. I thought, for sure, this dude was finally it. But in her sweet little southern voice, she said, "Honey, what if the Lord just gave you a way of escape? What makes you believe that boy's rejection isn't a blessing?"

Sure enough, she was right. Very soon after, his life ended up going a different direction, and I quickly realized how God spared me from a path that simply wasn't for me. God truly spared me from not only a road of suffering but also a road that simply wasn't for me. And thank goodness, because my husband is not only way better in every way but way hotter too. So, take *that*, football boy!

It's hard to view someone's rejection or God's "no" as a blessing, especially when it's something you truly wanted. Maybe it's a job you applied for, or a home you put an offer on, or even a relationship you desperately desired to work out. Rather than viewing rejection as misfortune, thank God in advance for a way of escape! He is always working behind the scenes and doing it for your good.

> God, if something is not Your will for me, give me a way of escape. Let things be made clear to me, even if it hurts. Amen.

# A Well-Rounded Life

*God ... richly provides us with
everything for our enjoyment.*
I TIMOTHY 6:17

One of the quotes I choose to live by is "Lighten up! There's so much joy in Jesus." However, I used to have notorious patterns of not "lightening up" at all. In fact, I would take myself so seriously, that I'd beat myself up if I fell short in any area of life. I put so much pressure on myself to be so perfectly well-rounded that when I failed, I'd get super whiny and cry-ey about it. It was so unrealistic, so silly; and as time went by, I started to realize that.

After having a conversation with one of my friends about this, she had the best advice. This is what she said to do:

Write everything you want to improve on a piece of paper.

Choose two topics that stand out the most.

Only focus on those two areas for the next two months.

The idea is that after two months of focus and consistency, you'll grow in confidence in those areas of weakness. Additionally, your former weaknesses will become second nature and part of your lifestyle, therefore, becoming your strengths.

In the Word of God, David was considered the weakest in his family. Everyone overlooked him and even considered him just a lowly shepherd boy. However, despite his age and weaknesses, David consistently practiced the use of a slingshot. He did this in order to protect the sheep from predators, and eventually, he became highly skilled. Because David was faithful in his "lowly" job, his slingshot skills allowed him to take down Goliath. And eventually, he become the king of all Israel.

Perfection will never be attainable. But if well-roundedness is your desire, consistency and prayer will help you achieve anything. Whether you desire to strengthen your spiritual walk, finances, marriage, fitness, parenting, friendships, nutrition, or professional life, God has already equipped you with the ability to do so.

The Lord doesn't expect perfection from us, but He takes delight in us reaching to Him for help. Pursue the things you're wanting to improve with joy and expectation. You can do all things through Christ who gives you strength!

> God, help me to choose two areas
> that You want me to improve in.
> Be with me on this journey and teach
> me things along the way. Amen.

# The Cycle Stops Here

*Therefore, if anyone is in Christ,
he is a new creation.
The old has passed away;
behold, the new has come.*
II CORINTHIANS 5:17 ESV

"Well, that's just the way I am. And if you don't like it, go cry me a river!" I've heard people say this, and quite frankly, I've said this before myself. We tend to justify the iffy parts of our personality simply because our parents were this way, or our grandparents were this way, or our ancestors were this way. It is what it is, and people should just get used to it! Right?

Goodness gracious, *no*!

One thing is true: we are a DNA combination of every good and bad character trait that has ever existed in our bloodline. We'd like to believe that the good parts of our character shine through us the most, but we cannot deny that generational curses exist.

God is constantly at work to transform our identity. Surrendering our hearts to Him makes us brand new; therefore, no matter how deep-rooted our tendencies are, Jesus gives us a chance to clean the slate. In God's Word, we see women who did just that:

Rahab was a prostitute. But because she feared the God of the Israelites, she aided Jewish spies in Jericho and vowed to leave her old lifestyle behind.

Ruth was born into an idol-worshipping family. But because of her loyalty to her mother-in-law, she converted her faith to the living God and moved to a land that worshipped Him.

Bathsheba had an affair. But because she suffered the shameful murder of her husband and the death of her firstborn son, she forsook that which was wrong and received unlimited grace.

Despite their mistakes and any curses from their lineage, these women chose to surrender to God completely, and every single one of them is found in the direct genealogy of Jesus Christ. What an honor!

Sometimes we need to destroy the reputation we've built for ourselves and let God's deliverance within us produce some real change. We must get bold, put our foot down, and say enough is *enough*! May every generational curse from your bloodline stop with you, and may it change the course of future generations.

> God, I pray that every cycle of addiction, debt, abuse, and brokenness be stopped with me, and not come anywhere near my children. Amen.

# The Seesaw and the Savior

*You are the light of the world.*

MATTHEW 5:14

I was just a little girl on the playground, teetering by myself on a seesaw (no idea how that's even possible, but I was doing it). In the middle of my loner-fest, the prettiest little girl walked up to me. I was stunned by her beauty, and goodness gracious, I couldn't believe she wanted to play with an awkward little freckle-faced kid like me. The moment Cristina joyfully sat at the other end of the seesaw, I immediately stopped feeling like a loser. Her kindness that day was the beginning of a bond that has lasted for nearly thirty years.

However, when we were in our twenties, I ran from the Lord. I was emotionally wounded by past abuses, dating someone who wasn't for me, and living far beneath what God intended. That is, until a package from Cristina arrived at my apartment. A devotional was inside that talked about being a beloved daughter of the King. As sweet as this gift was, seeing her words written on the inside cover profoundly and pivotally changed my life:

"I pray this devotional reminds you daily of who you are in Christ, and how He has great plans for you. I love you, friend."

She had no idea how timely this was, how vulnerable my heart was, and how ready I was to surrender; but God did. I broke down in tears, fell to my knees, and rededicated myself to Christ. Even though I was alone in my apartment, Cristina still showed up for me, just like she did when we were little girls. She saw my loneliness, stepped in joyfully as the friend I needed, and reminded me how valuable I was to her and to the kingdom of God.

We are all called to show up for the broken. We are all purposefully placed on this earth to love others and to point them to Jesus. It's so easy to feel like our own problems are too overwhelming to be there for others; however, that's exactly what Jesus did. He showed up for those who were teetering and lost and drew their hearts toward the Savior. How can you be a Cristina for someone today?

> God, let me be a light today for someone who needs You. Amen.

# "As for Me and My House," and Beyond

*But as for me and my house, we will serve the Lord.*

JOSHUA 24:15 ESV

Growing up, our mom faithfully taught my siblings and I about Jesus. We would sit groggily at the breakfast table, covered in eye boogers and bedhead, while she read us our daily devotional. We would sit in the back seat of our Suburban, rowdily teasing each other and making faces, while she prayed for us on our way to school. And when we arrived, she would always remind us of something that was very true, yet slightly creepy: "Remember, Jesus is always watching! He sees every thought, word, and action!"

That truth always felt so wild to me. Goodness gracious, it was almost like God was Santa Claus: He sees us when we're sleeping, He knows when we're awake, He knows if we've been bad or good, so be good for goodness' sake! *(I know you sang it, don't lie.)* As silly as that analogy was, it worked for me. My mom's reminder of God being all-knowing allowed me to develop a healthy desire to fear the Lord and do what was right.

Joshua 24:15 is a well-known and often recited verse. You can find "But as for me and my house, we will serve the Lord" on everything from wall art to casserole dishes. And we know the importance of serving God in our home, sharing the gospel with our children, and choosing to follow Him as a family. However, our "house" isn't just referring to the four walls we live in. It is also referring to our personal "house"—a.k.a. our mind, body, and soul. Our "house" is also our circles of influence—a.k.a. our workplace, community, and anywhere the Lord sends us. While our home address and family unit are the most important mission field, we are also called to serve the Lord in capacities that go beyond that. This requires great humility, obedience, and faith.

God wants to be a dweller. A dweller isn't just a visitor who gets kicked out when they overstay their welcome; a dweller remains present, 24/7. He wants to take precedence in our families, in our hearts, and in our mission fields. Let's always be conscious of His presence and allow Him to keep us accountable in the way we live in public and in private!

> God, dwell within me. Dwell within my home. Dwell within every area You want to send me. Amen.

# Worship Is Your Weapon

*Exalt the Lord our God, and worship at His footstool; Holy is He.*
PSALM 99:5 NASB1995

Worship music has always been like therapy for me. No matter what I was going through, turning on songs of praise would instantaneously change the atmosphere of my day and the way I felt. Music truly moved me, spoke to me, and drew me, so it wasn't entirely shocking that I married a musician.

Blaine truly is an incredible drummer. I must admit, he always looks so cute up there, being all rhythmic and rock star and stuff. (Goodness gracious, is it hot in here? No, just me?) I've watched him perform on national stages: from the Grand Ole Opry to *The Ellen DeGeneres Show* to the *Today* show to *American Idol*. However, no stage makes me prouder than watching him on the worship stage. The way he plays, the way he moves, and the way he uses his gift is so powerful each time, it moves me to tears.

Worship is powerful, and the Word of God proves it. One passage stands out to me the most and helps me understand why worship music has always been so healing for me. In II Chronicles 20:21-22, it says this:

*After consulting the people, Jehoshaphat appointed men to sing to the Lord and to praise Him for the splendor of His holiness as they went out at the head of the army, saying: "Give thanks to the Lord, for His love endures forever." As they began to sing and praise, the Lord set ambushes against the men of Ammon and Moab and Mount Seir who were invading Judah, and they were defeated.*

King Jehoshaphat used worship as a weapon. Before going into battle, he instructed the worshippers to stand on the front lines, ushering in the presence of God. And because he did this, the enemy was defeated.

When we praise the name of Jesus, it confuses the enemy. When we praise the name of Jesus, it ties his hands and forces him to flee. There is great power, security, and victory when we choose to worship ahead of every circumstance. Today, may your worship be a powerful weapon that immobilizes the enemy against any fiery darts that are trying to pierce your heart.

> God, may worship be my weapon.
> I will sing Your praises no matter
> what battle lies ahead. Amen.

# God, Where Are You?

*My ears had heard of You, but
now my eyes have seen You.*

JOB 42:5

When Blaine and I got engaged, we only had four months until the big day. It was quite a panicky feeling, but we were determined to make it happen. My mom and I immediately started dress shopping, and to my relief, we found *the* one. It was everything I ever dreamed of and more, but it needed alterations. I anxiously awaited the next few weeks with excited anticipation.

Finally, it was ready. I slipped it on and turned dramatically toward the mirror like an elegant princess. However, what I saw made me want to throw up. The dress was completely butchered, looking like a wonky white wrinkly washcloth. I wailed like a wounded walrus and told myself, "That's it. I'm postponing the wedding. I won't find another dress in time. My big day is ruined. God, where are you?" Goodness gracious, the drama.

Of course, God miraculously brought this whiny bride another dress just in time. It was beautiful, and I felt so foolish for expressing such unbelief. As minor as this situation was in the grand scheme of things, God showed me how He is always there, even in the small acts, even in the midst of my unbelief.

Just when we assume God has abandoned us, He finds new ways to draw us in. In fact, if we never went through difficult times, we would have no need for supernatural intervention. If we never needed to be rescued, we would have no need for a Savior.

In the Bible, many people desperately cried out to God during times when they felt like God was absent. David's circumstances were dire, and his emotional world was very broken. Yet, David praised God in the waiting, and God vindicated him greatly. Job literally lost everything—his family, his wealth, and even his health suffered. Yet, Job never denounced God, and everything he lost was restored in abundance and overflow.

God has never abandoned us, not once. Instead, He uses tough circumstances in our lives to teach us things, to help us unlearn things, and to build up our faith. No matter what, His presence is as apparent as the wind, blowing new life into our souls and revealing His mercies at every turn.

> God, I know You're there. Help me to trust You when my unbelief tries to take over. Amen.

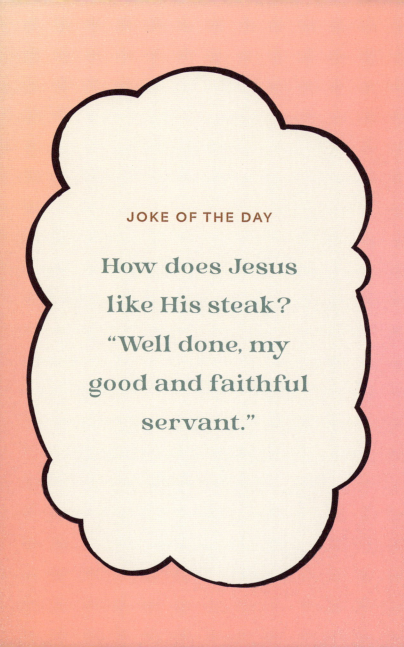

**JOKE OF THE DAY**

How does Jesus like His steak? "Well done, my good and faithful servant."

# An Orphaned Spirit

*I will not leave you as orphans;*
*I will come to you.*
JOHN 14:18

There was a time in my life when isolation felt easier. I preferred working alone over drama-mama settings. I preferred watching online sermons over suffering through small talk with "Gabbing Gabby," the church entrance greeter. I preferred keeping my problems to myself instead of hearing other opinions. Goodness gracious, every bit of human interaction irritated the fire out of me, and I took pride in living a stress-free independent life.

However, the root of my "lone-ranger-ness" stemmed from hurt. Abandonment, betrayal, bullying, and other abuses ripped the rug of trust from underneath me. I started to develop an orphaned spirit, where false perceptions of self-sufficiency and independence only led to vulnerability and overwhelm.

Today's generation is more interpersonally disconnected than ever before. Social media encourages us to engage behind a screen, reducing the need to engage in person. Online church services sufficiently edify us through a screen, reducing the need to be edified intimately with human interaction. Even the epidemic of offense has caused people to cut relationship ties with anyone who even slightly disagrees. The world fosters an orphaned spirit. However, there is great power in unity!

The Bible frequently references the Good Shepherd and His sheep. Even though sheep get cliquey, butt heads, and follow each other around doing dumb stuff, the Good Shepherd provides safety and protection for the flock against outside dangers. Yet, there is always one sheep with an orphaned spirit; this sheep wanders off alone, unintentionally making himself vulnerable for predators to attack, maim, and devour.

When we isolate ourselves, it's a dream come true for the enemy. If he can get you alone and separated from the pack, you become an open target. Sure, run-ins with people are inevitable, but the damage that the enemy inflicts during isolation is far more destructive. People aren't the enemy; the enemy is the enemy! God's plan for you is to live and serve effectively within His flock. You are not an orphan; you were bought with a price. Your Good Shepherd will stop at nothing to find you, rescue you from yourself, and lead you back into safety.

> God, I desire to thrive in community with my family, friends, and other believers. Heal me from past wounds and protect me from the threat of isolation. Amen.

# The Importance of Family

*For where two or three are gathered in
my name, there am I among them.*

MATTHEW 18:20 ESV

My childhood was precious. It was surrounded by love, blessing, and unity. Sure, my siblings and I fought, and yes, I might have called my brother an alien after accidentally busting his mouth open with a metal baseball bat, but that's neither here nor there (goodness gracious, poor guy).

Unfortunately, decades later, what felt like an unbreakable family unit crumbled when divorce struck. Abandonment, pain, and rejection wrecked us. The safety and stability I once knew as a little girl was ripped away as a young woman, leaving a trail of broken pieces and shattered hearts.

However, God used that circumstance to show me the true beauty of family. My in-laws stepped up as pillars of strength and prayer, our church family offered words of hope and encouragement, and now most of my family lives in the same neighborhood to support each other and do life together.

God wired us to be family-oriented beings with the desire to love and be loved. In fact, family is so important to Him, He gave us two:

An earthly family. This is the family we are born into. While not every family member walks with Christ, God's intention is for our earthly families to be balanced, whole, and a unit that serves the kingdom of God with unstoppable force.

A spiritual family. This is the family of fellow believers. Most times, our earthly family is a part of our spiritual family, but if not, God provides us with a spiritual family through church or ministry. In turn, our spiritual family greatly influences our earthly family, potentially leading those who are lost into the arms of Christ.

A godly family keeps you accountable amid mistakes. They provide wise counsel amid threats of temptation. They pour out support when your heart is crushed, and they express the kind of unconditional love that resembles the heart of Jesus.

Even if you have a dysfunctional earthly family, God desires you to embrace His gift of a spiritual family. No matter what, you have a heavenly Father who will never leave you, never forsake you, and who calls you His own forever.

> God, thank You for family. Help me to serve, love, and protect the earthly and spiritual family You've blessed me with. Amen.

# Why "Self-Love" Is Not the Answer

> *"Love the Lord your God with all your heart and with all your soul and with all your mind and with all your strength. The second is this: 'Love your neighbor as yourself.' There is no commandment greater than these."*
>
> MARK 12:30-31

I'm feeling a little feisty today, so buckle up, because I'm just going to say it:

If the "self-love" movement were a table, Jesus would have flipped it.

Whoa! Did your eyes widen when I said that? Hold on. Before you throw rotten tomatoes at me, let me explain.

Everywhere I look I see the word *self*: self-love, self-help, self-care, self-self-self all the time. Sure, caring for your body and mind is obvious. Yes, prioritizing your health is vital. However, there is something missing in most of these messages. Self-love leads us to believe that we are capable of artificially creating our own joy. It says that if we love ourselves enough, we can accomplish what we want in life all by ourselves. However, this false doctrine is a deceiver. It puts self on a pedestal, and historically it only causes more division in relationships with friends, family, and within the body of Christ.

The overwhelming presence of self will always be a hindrance to the overwhelming presence of God. We will never be able to heal ourselves or love ourselves the way Jesus can. Despite what some say, focusing primarily on self will only lead to confusion and friction within our perceptions, relationships, and life. Leaning on God for all our wants and needs is always the answer.

When we pursue Christ, it helps us understand how passionately loved we are by Him. It reminds us that He is God, and we can rely on Him as our ultimate source of unwavering love—a love that we could never provide for ourselves no matter how hard we try.

> God, I want less of me and more of You. Help me to find the balance of loving You, loving others, and loving who You created me to be. Amen.

# Spirit vs. Emotion

*In the same way, the Spirit helps us in our weakness. We do not know what we ought to pray for, but the Spirit Himself intercedes for us through wordless groans.*

ROMANS 8:26

Have you ever wanted something so badly, even though it wasn't right for you? Sometimes we have desires that burn so hotly within us that we stop at nothing to get what we want. We even justify our feelings by going as far as saying, "I believe God wants me to have this," when in reality we're just being greedy and infatuated little stinkers who are confusing our human emotions with Spirit-led guidance.

Goodness gracious, y'all, I have been there and done that! I remember believing it was God's will for me to have a mermaid tail, but that was just my desires. I remember believing it was God's will for me to be on *Barney*, but that was just my desires. I remember believing it was God's will for me to have a career in journalism, but that was just my desires. I confused my emotions with the God's voice; and in order to make things abundantly clear for me, He slammed those doors shut. Lovingly, of course.

Hear me out: emotions and feelings are *not* bad! They are God-given, and many times He uses the big emotions we feel as an opportunity to draw us closer to Him. However, we must be careful; having discernment allows God's Spirit to influence good decision-making rather than allowing our emotions to lead to mistakes.

Emotions lie, but the Holy Spirit guides; and He will never lead us to compromise. Sorry not sorry, but God will never tell us to spend all our money on designer bags, sell our bodies on OnlyFans, or date married people. No, friend: His Spirit will always guide us to be wise, holy, and influential for the kingdom of God.

We must become emotionally healthy enough to separate our feelings from our faith. Today, carefully study God's Word for guidance. Seek counsel from God-fearing mentors who have your best interests in mind. And lastly, evaluate your "gut feelings"—are they justifying your humanly desires or are they pointing you to Christ?

> God, I don't want my infatuations to
> lead me into dark places.
> I desire Your Spirit to always lead
> me into righteousness. Amen.

# Social Media: Menace or Ministry?

*Have nothing to do with foolish, ignorant controversies; you know that they breed quarrels. And the Lord's servant must not be quarrelsome but kind to everyone, able to teach, patiently enduring evil.*

II TIMOTHY 2:23-24 ESV

The internet is a weird place. We consume information, share our thoughts, and communicate with others online. Being that I spend most of my time on social media for work, I've seen it all: the good, the bad, and the ugly that is associated with interacting on every platform.

One day, I decided to do a humorous video highlighting the phrase: "Pray before you post, because being petty don't make you pretty!" It got a lot of laughs, lots of shares among friends, and lots of *"amens"* in the comments section. Because goodness gracious, it's so true! How often do we see people's online activity and cringe—or rather, how often do we look back on our own activity and cringe ourselves?

Proverbs 18:21 says life and death are in the power of the tongue. Not only does that refer to the words we speak, but it also refers to the words we type. Chiming in in the comments section with disapproval or rage never works, never makes anything better, and never changes anyone's mind. Not only that, but people are also watching. If the things we post or the comments we share don't align with God's Spirit, it becomes a bad witness for those who view from the sidelines. I know, it's hard, and sometimes it's important to speak up or speak out against something. In this case, do it the biblical way: if you have a problem with someone, go directly to them instead of airing dirty laundry online and shooting venomous verbal arrows for the whole world to see.

It's time for us to start being warriors for the kingdom of God instead of being warriors in the comments section. Ask God to reveal your motives before posting. Is the intention to speak life or to stir discord? Is it aimed to promote peace, or is it a passive-aggressive jab toward someone else?

We can choose to use social media as a menace, or we can choose to use it as a ministry. In this day in age, we must choose wisely.

> God, I vow to use social media as a ministry and nothing else. Amen.

# The Three C's

*In his hand is the life of every living thing
and the breath of all mankind.*
JOB 12:10 ESV

Ever since I was a little girl, I had this burning desire to do something spectacular. I wanted my legacy to be fossilized like a dinosaur foot, stamped clearly enough for future generations to say, "Look! That goofy lady was here, and she actually made a difference!"

But like everyone, the heaviness of life landed square on my noggin, falling from the sky like an anvil in *Looney Tunes*. This little girl got bullied. This teenager got her heart broken. This young adult walked through abuse. The star-shaped, rose-colored glasses I viewed the world through must have changed prescriptions, because goodness gracious, it was hard enough to see straight, let alone do something as farfetched as change the world.

Yet, during some of the darkest times in my life, a dear family friend named Dr. Judy Laird would always remind me of the three C's:

There are things we don't CAUSE. We live in a fallen world, and things will happen that aren't our fault.

There are things we cannot CONTROL. But when we place full control into the hands of Jesus, our faith allows Him to work all things out for our good.

There are things we cannot CHANGE. However, even though pain weaves itself through our life's frayed and imperfect tapestry, God's mercy never changes.

Through the heartache, He is good.

Through the mistakes, He is good.

Through the uh-oh's and what-the-heck's and I-can't-do-this-anymore's, He is good.

Maybe you feel me here. Maybe joy was ripped so violently out of your life that restoration seems laughable. If so, let me tell you something: your mess isn't big enough to freak God out, and it's certainly not big enough to stop Him from pursuing you. You were born with purpose, on purpose, and for a purpose so massive you'd spit your hazelnut coffee out of your nose.

Finding God allows you to find yourself, and finding Him makes your purpose clear. Therefore, when bumps in the road happen, peace allows you to not take everything so doggone seriously. Lighten up, friends! There truly is so much joy in Jesus!

*God, I choose to smile, take a deep breath, and remember the three C's. I know that no matter what, You are for me. Amen.*

# Unclutter Your Heart

*But all things should be done decently and in order.*
I CORINTHIANS 14:40 ESV

When I heard "cleanliness is next to godliness" was actually *not* a verse in the Bible, I did a little victory dance. I suddenly didn't feel so bad about the "forts" my kids created, the un-closable closet doors stuffed with garage-sale-worthy junk, the sixteen water cups sitting by my bedside, or the mildewy laundry I accidentally left in the washer for four days. However, it's funny: the moment I decide to unclutter the things around me, I legit feel like a superwoman.

Let's be real: when our house is chaotic, we are unproductive. When things are too loud in the car, we can't hear ourselves think. When our hearts are cluttered with bad memories, we are miserable. And goodness gracious, as hard as we try to justify our messiness with "just being human," living a cluttered life never serves us well.

Scripture talks about order often, and pursuing order always brings balance within our hearts and minds. When we choose to do some "inner spring cleaning" and remove things within our lives that don't belong, it makes room for God to fill us with His goodness. Order brings clarity, improves relationships, sharpens communication, and ushers in an atmosphere of peace. In fact, Mother Teresa once said:

*"A clean heart can see God, can speak to God, and can see the love of God in others."*

Uncluttering our hearts, minds, and spirit allows us to hear God clearly, ponder on things that are true, and produce excellence that overflows in every area of our lives.

Today, I'd like you to do something:

Take a piece of paper and write a column of three things *in your home* that need to be organized.

Then, in a separate column, write down three things *in your heart or mind* that need to be cleaned out.

Choose one thing from each category and focus on uncluttering those two things this week.

There is always grace, friends. God, in His mercy, knows your circumstances, and He is right there with you in the middle of your mess. Even so, He has also given you the strength and ability to unclutter your life. Walk in order and walk in freedom!

> God, I choose order today. Help me unclutter the things that don't belong. Amen.

# Boldness, Persecution, and X-rated Material

*Be on your guard; stand firm in the faith; be courageous; be strong. Do everything in love.*

I CORINTHIANS 16:13-14

Jesus never said being a believer would be easy. In fact, He said we would face inevitable pushback, hatred, and persecution just for being a Christian. I never fully understood what that felt like until June 24, 2022. That day, I posted a lighthearted video expressing my views on a subject that I believe most Christians would agree with, and goodness gracious, the fiery darts were launched from every direction. People cursed me in the comments, sent death threats in my DM's, and I was even mailed an anonymous hate package of X-rated material. Yes, that really happened. No, I have no idea how they got my address. And yes, I was slightly freaked out.

I called my husband and told him about the package. But the more we discussed it, the more we found the humor in it. My fear started to fade into an emboldened "whatever, it's all good." Since I knew the heart behind my post was pure, I trusted God to sustain me and my family no matter what.

Eventually, courage and security flooded my entire being. I grabbed my phone, logged onto Instagram, and boldly told my audience that my fear of God would always supersede any shallow fear of people's pushback. Because of obedience and fearless faith, God opened floodgates of blessings—my number of subscribers more than doubled, business opportunities came out of the woodwork, and godly relationships flourished. It was over-the-top awesome.

Even though standing up for what's right can be scary, the disobedience of remaining quiet is even scarier. People are desperate for goodness and truth, and there is no one more fitting to shine the light of Jesus to your friends than you.

Find a way to boldly include Christ in your daily life: in your job, in your interactions, in your circles of influence. He gave you life so you can unashamedly give Him glory in return. May the days of playing small, staying silent, and leaving out the name of Jesus to keep others comfortable be over for you! Be unafraid of pushback, kick fear to the curb, and stand for biblical truth in love. Today, step out in faith and obedience, and boldly proclaim His name!

> Jesus, You were unashamed to bear my sins on the cross; therefore, I will be unashamed to tell others of Your goodness. Give me supernatural boldness today. Amen.

# The Forgiveness Cure

*And whenever you stand praying, forgive,
if you have anything against anyone, so
that your Father also who is in heaven
may forgive you your trespasses.*

MARK 11:25 ESV

There have been times in my life where I was justified in my anger. During the mental anguish and inner torment, my body would start to suffer physically. Fatigue, sickness, and stomach pains would arrive in ghastly proportions. (Or should I say, "gas-ly" proportions? Totally not joking, either. Unforgiveness can absolutely lead to diarrhea.)

However, forgiveness is a healer. The moment I chose to let things go, like *for real*, I started feeling better not just emotionally but physically. Forgiving those who aren't sorry allows God to heal the depths of our souls and even our bodies. Forgiveness changes us, and changing our own hearts causes a ripple effect that results in change within the hearts of others.

Jesus took on every anguish, every trauma, and every hurt we've ever experienced in the past, present, and future. He bore it all in an agonizing death on the cross, just because He loves us so much. I have learned that no matter what, God is *for me* no matter what happens *to me*. I have learned that I am not a victim, I am a victor and more than a conqueror.

I have learned that living in unforgiveness is like drinking poison while hoping the other person will somehow suffer. I have learned to believe the Word when it says there may be pain in the night, but joy comes in the morning (see Psalm 30:5).

Is it hard to forgive and let go? Goodness gracious, yes! But choosing to remain in bondage is much, much harder. Releasing the chokehold of hurt will open you up to magnificent favor and purpose in your life. You make a difference in the lives of others in much greater ways once you choose to leave the bondage of your past behind.

God has His eye on you. He has seen your pain and wants to free you from it. He desires to hold you in His arms, whisper how much He loves you, and remind you that since He has forgiven you, you can forgive others too.

> God, I choose to forgive. Even if I must forgive multiple times a day, I will. Give me joy and give me strength.
> Amen.

# When Nothing Is Going Right

*The Lord is not slow to fulfill his promise as some count slowness, but is patient toward you, not wishing that any should perish, but that all should reach repentance.*

II PETER 3:9 ESV

There are those days where nothing is going right. You try to make coffee, but the only one left is the gross store brand. You try to iron a shirt, but that wrinkle in the shape of a lightning bolt refuses to flatten out. You hear your kid say, "I just farted in my cereal!" so you sprint to dump it out over fear of pink eye. Goodness gracious, even the beautiful things in life are irritating, like "Why does that flower have to be extra pretty and flawless today? Ugh. Show-off."

I'm sure reading all those things makes you giggle inside. But experiencing it in real time doesn't feel funny at all, huh? Thankfully, I have good news: there is a cure to escaping irritation when it creeps up. It's not a pill, it's not a cream, it's not a spa day complete with limitless chocolate and cucumber-infused water and people telling you how perfect you are in every way (though, that would be nice).

Instead, there is an ultimate cure. The soothing balm of the Word of God gently releases feelings of irritation and provides a comforting barrier of protection around our emotionally fickle souls. And in turn, out of the abundance of our hearts, our mouths will speak words and reactions that exude patience, mercy, and joy in every circumstance.

Feelings of irritation will happen. Yet, in spite of us, He extends grace and mercy even on our most unattractive days. He desires to change the way we see things, the way we react to things, and the way we feel as a whole. Like a child, our Father listens to our tantrums, holds us until we calm down, and lovingly teaches us how to be better witnesses for Him.

In your quiet time, tell God exactly how you've been feeling. If the day was rough, tell Him about the things that irritate you most. Ask Him to pour an oil of healing over every part of your heart, and vow to release all your stressors to Him.

> God, I don't want irritation to take over.
> Let my presence, reactions, and life
> exude a peacemaking spirit. Amen.

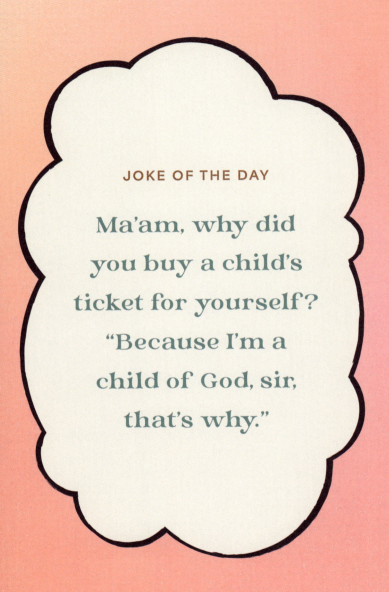

**JOKE OF THE DAY**

Ma'am, why did you buy a child's ticket for yourself? "Because I'm a child of God, sir, that's why."

# Contentment: Our Gift to God

*But godliness with contentment is great gain.*
I TIMOTHY 6:6 ESV

Confession: I have an infatuation with scrolling through Zillow. Apparently, I'm not the only one, because *Saturday Night Live* did a whole skit on this. But truly, I can't help it, guys. My toxic trait is that I like to pretend I'm a lottery winner and have the pick of the litter on any multimillion-dollar mansion available in our area. Childish of me? *Absolutely.*

Even though our home is wonderful, Blaine still has to put up with my house-hunting fantasies. Every time I send him a Zillow link, he just sighs and rolls his eyes: "What's wrong with *our* house? We have a *great* house. I *like* our house. You need to be *content* with *our house*!" And yes, he is annoyingly right.

In the Bible, God's people experienced discontentment often. They murmured about Moses' leadership, even after he delivered them from slavery. They complained about their food, even after God miraculously provided it from heaven. And then, those little brats had the *audacity* to *whine* when God disciplined them for their ungrateful hearts! Goodness gracious, you'd think that after *all* the miracles the Israelites had witnessed, after *all* the signs and wonders they had seen, and after *all* the answered prayers they were living out they'd be content, but they *weren't*.

Listen, guys: we are guilty of the same thing, sometimes daily! God has given us many gifts, and He has provided us everything we need in this life. However, contentment isn't His gift to us; it's our gift to Him. When we accept every blessing, both big and small, it allows us to see how well taken care of we are by our heavenly Father. When we choose contentment, it also reminds us that we are currently living out many answered prayers from our past.

Even though contentment is the greatest form of gratitude, sometimes God allows discontentment in your life to identify things you need to change. Whether it's discontentment in your physical state, emotional well-being, or spiritual life, God wants you to lay those concerns at His feet. Ask Him for wisdom on how to make good changes and praise Him in the process.

> God, I am so grateful and content for everything You've done for me thus far. Remind me of my answered prayers and refine me when necessary. Amen.

# A Rich Spiritual Inheritance

*I am reminded of your sincere faith,
a faith that dwelt first in your grandmother
Lois and your mother Eunice and now,
I am sure, dwells in you as well.*
II TIMOTHY 1:5 ESV

My kids hit the jackpot in the grandma department. Their Meme and Honey are legit queens: they love God, adore our children, and live just minutes from our house. (Can I get an amen on that one?) Listen, we aren't ashamed to admit that their closeness has spoiled us rotten. But goodness gracious, can you blame us for loving free babysitting?

Our mothers are not flashy, not wealthy, and both have faced incredible hardships. Yet, they are fully committed to their greatest calling in life, which is pointing their children to Jesus. Because of this, we are recipients of a rich spiritual inheritance that far surpasses any amount of money, power, or worldly gain.

I firmly believe that our greatest purpose in life is to spiritually impact the next generation. In the Bible, Timothy's mother (Eunice) and grandmother (Lois) understood this assignment. They took full responsibility for raising Timothy in the ways of the Lord, and diligently instilled the Word of God into his spirit. Without fully knowing their impact, Timothy's mom and grandma prepared him for a future in ministry that ultimately shaped Christianity forever. The spiritual inheritance they gave their boy was eternal and priceless.

We have all been given a spiritual inheritance by God, yet few of us know how to make deposits and withdrawals from this heavenly trust fund. In order to receive our inheritance and pass it down to our children, we must surrender our lives to God and allow Him to work through us.

Jesus's heart for children was unmatched. He poured into them, listened to them, and referred to them constantly. We must match His heart! Today, ask God to reveal how you can be a role model that provides a rich spiritual inheritance for the next generation.

> God, I desire to unlock my spiritual inheritance and impart it to the children after me. Amen.

# As Good As It Gets

*And we all, with unveiled face,
beholding the glory of the Lord,
are being transformed into
the same image from one degree
of glory to another.*
II CORINTHIANS 3:18 ESV

I've said this before, but my husband is a rock star. No really, he actually is—that boy has played drums for artists all over the world (and goodness gracious, he sure looks delicious doing it). His parents sacrificed greatly for him to pursue this dream, and finally, Blaine landed gigs on national television. His parents were overjoyed; watching their baby boy experience such success made their support, investments, and selflessness all worthwhile.

However, reaching that peak wasn't as satisfying as Blaine had hoped. He felt deflated and empty, thinking *"Welp, I guess this as good as it gets."* While lying alone in his hotel room, Blaine prayed that God would fill the void in his heart and, if it be His will, to bring him a wife. Soon after, I came into the picture, and to this day, God continues to take Blaine from glory to glory.

In the Bible, Job had it all—wealth, family, and unshakable faith. It seemed like life couldn't get any better, until Job lost it all. His children perished, his wealth was drained, and his wife begged him to curse God and die. However, Job's faith never left. He believed God's goodness would eventually intervene, and sure enough, it did. Job's wealth doubled, he had more children, his wife's heart softened, and he was spiritually transformed forever.

Sometimes when we have mountaintop experiences, an underlying fear creeps in of, *"Welp, now that I've made it, all that's left is to tumble back down."* However, that is simply a lie! We will experience valleys, yes. But God promises that we will go from glory to glory, and one mountaintop experience will always lead to another when we choose to walk with Him.

It's fun to reflect on the glory days. However, success will never fully satisfy us; only God can. He pulls us out of every crevice and leads us up mountaintops more glorious than the ones before. When we stay in step with God, our latter days will be greater than our former. The best is still yet to come!

**God, lead the way in the mountain ranges of my life. Amen.**

# Things God Cannot Do

*In the hope of eternal life, which God, who does not lie, promised before the beginning of time.*

TITUS 1:2

My mom recently bought a house in my neighborhood, which was one of the most exciting days of my life. After years of living nearly eight hours away, my mom could finally cook me dinner and babysit my kids and organize my house, including my atomic bomb of a pantry. (Just kidding. Actually no, not kidding at all.)

The house she found was perfect, and the inspection showed it was in excellent shape. The former owners said they never experienced any issues with the house, and repetitively bragged about their honesty. However, their constant talk about their integrity was unsettling. I mean, goodness gracious, truly honest people don't usually brag about being honest people, if you know what I mean.

Sure enough, upon moving in, my mom started having plumbing issues. Tee-tee and poo-poo were constantly bubbling up from the drains, toilets, and sinks. Sure enough, my mom discovered that the plumbing was severely corroded, and apparently, the former owners *knew this*, and *simply chose to never use toilet paper*. First of all, gross; second of all, the red flags were correct.

There is something to be said about a person who is full of integrity with every word and intention of the heart. Sometimes, the idea of telling a white lie feels like the only solution to avoiding disaster or to get what we want. However, even the tiniest deception goes against God's character. And because He sees the depths of our hearts and motives, God cannot bless manipulation and dishonesty in any way, shape, or form. God's character is revealed through three things He simply cannot do:

He cannot lie.
He cannot fail.
He is never late.

God is a man of His word, He always pulls through, and He does it just in time. As His children, we must embrace these character traits too. Any time we are tempted to get out of a sticky situation by bending the truth, bailing out, or not keeping our word, God's Spirit always raises a red flag within our spirit. We must remain faithful and truthful; these character traits will always result in blessing!

> God, I want Your character. I want to always be truthful, dependable, and a woman of my word. Amen.

# Gabbin' and Gossipin'

*In the same way, women are to be worthy of respect, not malicious talkers but temperate and trustworthy in everything.*

I TIMOTHY 3:11

There are two kinds of people. The first is the kind of person who never says a bad word about anyone. Their demeanor is that of a teddy bear, their heart is as soft as a baby's butt, and their trustworthiness is that of a bank vault. The second, however, is the kind of person you can't say a word to. That is, unless you want your business to be broadcasted to your entire hometown and headlined on the local news. All of us have either been guilty of gabbin' and gossipin,' or we've painfully been the victim of it.

It is so hard for people to embrace how wrong gossiping is. I've heard people excuse it by saying things like, "I'm not saying this to gossip, I'm saying this so we can pray." Goodness gracious, it's almost like the juiciness of others' lives makes us feel slightly better about our own dysfunction. However, gossip is something God detests.

When we take a harder look at Scripture, the Lord condemns gossip with an iron fist. He lumps gossips into the same category as people who are murderers and haters of God. That may sound a bit dramatic, but since there is absolutely nothing kind or uplifting about gossip, it's not too far-off of a claim.

Gossip and slander diminishes the person who is the subject of the conversation, while simultaneously corroding the character of the one who is speaking it. Before talking about someone's misfortune or "innocently" taking part in hearing about it, consider these things first:

Is this conversation constructive?
Is this conversation encouraging?
Is this conversation pleasing to God?

If the answer is no to any of those three questions, self-control must come into play—both on the speaking end and on the listening end. No matter what, the Lord equally loves the person we're tempted to talk about just as much as He loves us. May our words about others always uplift, encourage, and be pleasing to the ears of God!

*God, give me self-control when I'm tempted to gossip, and give me the courage to stop it before it starts. Amen.*

# God, Why?

*For I am convinced that neither death nor life ... will be able to separate us from the love of God that is in Christ Jesus our Lord.*

ROMANS 8:38-39

One of the first questions my father-in-law ever asked me was, "How old are you?"

"Twenty-three," I replied.

He guffawed and threw his head back, "I have underwear older than you. *On!*"

That sealed the deal for me. I liked Blaine, *and* I liked his dad. Goodness gracious, what a win-win!

Neville loved us. He led us through highs and cradled us through lows. He stepped in as a father when I needed one the most. We even named our son after him. So when he passed away unexpectedly, we were crushed.

We questioned God. Why did the hospital mishandle him so poorly? Why did my husband lose his hero? Why did my God-fearing mother-in-law have to be widowed so suddenly? Why did my sister-in-law have to witness him slip away like that? And why did he have to take his last breath on our daughter's seventh birthday? Negative thoughts entered our minds: "God isn't good. He doesn't love you. If that were true, this would've never happened."

We understand the pain of not knowing why. It makes us feel vulnerable, resentful, and out of control. If we don't know why, how can we cope?

Put simply, we don't know why things happen the way they do, but we do know God turns our pain into purpose. We don't know why we suffer, but we do know Jesus suffered on our behalf. We don't know why we face certain hardships in our lifetime, but we do know we were born for such a time as this. Adam and Eve chose disobedience, yet God chose to save mankind anyway. And ultimately, we have a choice, too:

- A choice to accept the freedom through a relationship with Jesus or a choice not to.
- A choice to receive the hope of eternal life or a choice not to.
- A choice to believe that God's plans for our life are always good or a choice not to.

Choosing Jesus guarantees that one day, we will know the why. Until that day, I can promise you this: nothing will separate you from the love of Christ. Ever.

> I choose You, Jesus. I choose to believe You work all things together for my good. Amen.

# What Does 3-in-1 Even Mean?

*And when Jesus was baptized, immediately he went up from the water, and behold, the heavens were opened to him, and he saw the Spirit of God descending like a dove and coming to rest on him; and behold, a voice from heaven said, "This is my beloved Son, with whom I am well pleased."*

MATTHEW 3:16-17 ESV

As a kid, it was hard to grasp the concept of the Trinity: God the Father, God the Son, and God the Holy Spirit. My six-year-old brain just didn't get it. How could the Father be the Son, while also being … a *ghost*? I mean, goodness gracious, the only 3-in-1 thing I knew about was that large bottle of Suave in our shower.

I get it; the concept of three beings acting as one doesn't compute in our mortal minds. But throughout my journey in God's Word, I've learned something:

*God's choice to be 3-in-1 proves that He is everywhere all at once—it proves His omnipresence. From the beginning of time, He has never abandoned humanity. God the Father walked with Adam in the garden, God the Son walked with man on earth, and God the Spirit walks with us today.*

It was a light bulb moment. There has never been a second, *not one*, where God wasn't with us. If that's not love, I don't know what is.

God gave us life, Jesus gave us freedom, and the Holy Spirit gave us direct access to the Creator of the universe. The cross bridged the gap between us and God, and now the Holy Spirit is able to lead us, guide us, and direct us in making right choices. Additionally, because of the Holy Spirit, we don't need to do anything special to speak to God. We don't need to sacrifice animals, burn offerings, or go through a spiritual leader to have our requests made known. The Holy Spirit intercedes on our behalf, and His "gut-feeling-whispers" always point us in the right direction: financially, relationally, professionally, physically, emotionally, and spiritually.

There is nothing God loves more than humanity. His "3-in-1-ness" made it possible to always be there for us throughout every moment in time. What security and confidence it brings to know that He has never left us lonely!

> God, thank You for always being there.
> I especially thank You for allowing
> me to experience the gift of the Holy
> Spirit in my lifetime. Amen.

# Guarding the Gates

*I will not set before my eyes anything that is worthless. I hate the work of those who fall away; it shall not cling to me.*

PSALM 101:3 ESV

One of my all-time favorite songs in Sunday school was this gem:

*"Oh be careful little eyes what you see, oh be careful little eyes what you see. For the Father up above is looking down in love. Oh be careful little eyes what you see."*

The song repeats with verses on being careful with what we listen to, what we say, and where we go. And, annoyingly, my mom referred to this song as to why we weren't allowed to watch PG-13 movies or listen to "secular boy bands." Instead, our entire entertainment library only consisted of things like *VeggieTales*, *The Power Team*, Steven Curtis Chapman, and Carman. Goodness gracious, what icons.

Before you say we were deprived, we weren't. Childhood is the one era I'm most proud of and the one era I genuinely love reflecting upon. As strict as she was, my mom did what any good parent should do: guard the gates of a child's fragile soul. Because of this, it protected us from being introduced to things too young. My mother knew that when things are prematurely awakened in a child via the things they see or hear, it can cause irreparable damage.

Not only is this true for our children, but this is also true for us. Everything we see, hear, and consume plants something within our spirit. When we allow our eyes to watch horror movies or pornography, we give the enemy direct access to sow fear and perversion into our souls. When we allow our ears to hear sexualized music filled with cursing and violence, we give the enemy direct access to sow torment and distortion into our souls. It numbs us, it desensitizes us, and it draws us further and further from the things of the Lord.

Let's examine the things we're letting in today. What are we allowing to enter our ear gate and our eye gate? Stand guard, be alert, for ourselves, and our children!

> God, I vow to protect my ear gate and my eye gate. I want nothing to defile my heart or mind. Lead me and convict me in every situation. Amen.

# Charlie and the Smoky Hotel Room

*And we all, who with unveiled faces
contemplate the Lord's glory,
are being transformed.*

II CORINTHIANS 3:18

I'm such a sucker for hearing stories about transformation. It makes me so giddy and giggly, and today, I have a feeling you'll appreciate it too.

There once was a man named Charlie. He was prideful, mean, and an alcoholic. He ran from God; yet, he had a family who continuously prayed for his salvation behind the scenes, including his own daughter.

One night, after drinking, he hit the road for a work trip. Normally, he would listen to music as he drove; but for some reason, he played sermons instead. For hours, unbeknownst to Charlie, the gospel of Jesus Christ slowly softened his heart. After arriving at his hotel, still drunk and emotionally conflicted, Charlie turned on the television. The channel landed on the face of a man named Billy, who spoke so personally that Charlie felt like they were talking face-to-face.

Billy told Charlie about redemption. He told him about God's overwhelming forgiveness. He told Charlie that Jesus could take all his mistakes and failures and use them for good. Then, a girl named Dolly walked on screen and started to sing. After hearing her first musical note, Charlie crumbled.

For the very first time, Charlie felt the tangible presence of the Holy Spirit. With raised arms, a tear-streaked face, and transformed heart, Charlie wept as Dolly sang: "He's alive! He's alive! He's alive, and I'm forgiven, Heaven's gates are opened wide!"

From that moment on, Charlie was never the same. He dedicated his life to Jesus and never touched alcohol again. His daughter was so overwhelmed that every painful memory she had of her father was erased by forgiveness. Charlie was free, forever changed, and the mere mention of Jesus's name still brings him to tears.

The cool part?

Charlie ... is my grandfather.

His daughter ... is my mom.

Dolly ... is Dolly Parton.

And Billy ... was Billy Graham.

Goodness gracious, God truly has no limits. Whether it's in the sanctuary of a church or in a smoky hotel room, God's Spirit will meet you where you are. Never stop praying, and never underestimate the healing power of the Savior!

> God, I anticipate Your presence to show up unexpectedly. Move in my heart and in the hearts around me. Amen.

# A Life of Freedom

*In Him, you also, after listening to the message of truth, the gospel of your salvation—having also believed, you were sealed in Him with the Holy Spirit of promise.*
**EPHESIANS 1:13 NASB1995**

What a life-changing time this has been. My prayer, friend, is that these ninety entries filled you with hope, that they filled you with newfound purpose, that you have grown to understand just who you are in Christ Jesus. His plan for you is to step into your calling with boldness and with a smile on your face. May everything that has hindered you in the past be stripped away. Those who laugh, last—so let's all learn to not take life so seriously! You were given such a beautiful life by such a loving Father. There is so much freedom in joy, so much freedom in truth, and so much freedom in Jesus.

As we close, let me pray over you:

*Father, I speak life over (insert your name here) today. I declare right now that she walks in perfect step with You. I thank You in advance that she is healed, that she is delivered, that she is made whole in every way: physically, emotionally, and spiritually. I pray she develops a hunger for You that satiates her* innermost being, so much so that she will be a difference maker for Your kingdom. I speak unity within her family, favor in her relationships, and protection over her children or future children. May (insert your name here) surrender her heart to You and live a life that is pleasing unto You from this day forward. I pray all these things in the mighty, powerful, wonderful name of Jesus, Amen.

If you've never received Jesus as your personal Lord and Savior, or if you're unsure if heaven is your final destination, then pray this prayer out loud:

Dear God, I believe. I believe Jesus died for me, rose again, and is seated at Your right hand. I know I have been bought with a price. A life with You is so much sweeter than one without You—therefore, I give You my life today. In Jesus's name, amen!

I can't wait to hear your testimonies. Find me on social media, girlfriend.

And goodness gracious, you are so cute when you smile. Don't you ever forget it!

—xoxo, *Hannah Crews*

*Dear Friend,*

This book was prayerfully crafted with you, the reader, in mind. Every word, every sentence, every page was thoughtfully written, designed, and packaged to encourage you—right where you are this very moment. At DaySpring, our vision is to see every person experience the life-changing message of God's love. So, as we worked through rough drafts, design changes, edits, and details, we prayed for you to deeply experience His unfailing love, indescribable peace, and pure joy. It is our sincere hope that through these Truth-filled pages your heart will be blessed, knowing that God cares about you—your desires and disappointments, your challenges and dreams.

*He knows. He cares. He loves you unconditionally.*

**BLESSINGS!**
**THE DAYSPRING BOOK TEAM**

---

Additional copies of this book and
other DaySpring titles can be purchased
at fine retailers everywhere.
Order online at <u>dayspring.com</u>
or
by phone at 1-877-751-4347